The Depression Advantage

Tom Wootton

Bipolar Advantage, Publishers
San Francisco

The Depression Advantage

www.BipolarAdvantage.com
www.DepressionAdvantage.com

Many of the names and even genders in this book have been
changed in order to respect privacy. Internet addresses given
in this book were accurate at the time the book went to press.

© 2007 by Tom Wootton

Cover design by Don Farnsworth
www.magnoliaeditions.com

ISBN 978-0-9774423-2-4

Table of Contents

Preface

This book is about spiritual growth and the role that depression can play in it. Central to that growth is learning how to change our behavior so that we can have better relationships with others.

If you are honest with yourself, you have to admit that it is only tough times that give us a strong enough desire to change ourselves. Depression gave me the unbearable feeling that I need to do anything I can to change myself into a better person.

Please don't misunderstand; depression is far from some kind of sign that a person is not acting right, or some kind of punishment for his behavior. Depression is a real and horrible mental illness, that in the case of clinical depression, often has nothing at all to do with our circumstances in life.

However, that does not mean that we cannot find lessons in it. I believe that facing depression gave me the insight to see that true spiritual growth should be measured by how I am acting in my day-to-day encounters with others. My own "Dark Night of the Soul" was the most important step in becoming who I am today.

"I have come to measure spiritual advancement, not alone by the light that surrounds one when he meditates or by the visions he has of saints, but by what he is able to endure in the hard, cold light of day.[1]" This has been my favorite quote for some time, but I now include how we react to things as part of how we endure; an insight that was until recently not clear to me.

While the focus of much of this book is the similarity of experience in depression and mystical experience, more important is the result of such experiences. Any true advantage in depression must by definition have better behavior as a major outcome. I believe the changes in my actions, as judged by those around me, have proven that I have begun to find the Depression Advantage and put it into action.

As part of writing this book, I created a new talk based on the ideas outlined later in *Redefining Our Scale*. I have found that people are very open to looking at depression in a different way. I have been approached by many people who say that their experiences have been similar and have also begun to see depression in a whole new light. I hope you can find it in yourself to look for a new way to "see" depression too.

I fully believe in the possibility of turning depression into an advantage. I think I have made some great strides in the right direction. As I learn more about myself through depression, I look forward to the day when my actions will

---

1 Sri Gyanamata, God Alone: The Life and Letters of a Saint, page 181. Los Angeles: Self Realization Fellowship, 1984

always demonstrate my insight. That will be a glorious day indeed.

Introduction

I can trace my undiagnosed bipolar condition as far back as nine years old. In my youth, the symptoms were almost entirely hypomanic (lots of energy, very little sleep, etc.) with minor periods of depression, consisting of mostly just low energy. By the time I was thirty years old, my bipolar condition had settled into a predictable pattern. I would work with practically no sleep for nine months, then quit my job and hang out at the beach or in bed for three months. It was easy for me to confuse that pattern with the school system's summer break schedule, so I thought it was normal.

Twenty years ago, I moved to a monastery because my spiritual interest had become the most important thing in my life. I can trace my strong interest in a meditative life to the age of two, when I became fascinated with watching my breath go in and out. I read about, contemplated, and meditated about spiritual matters my whole life; it was the only thing that mattered to me.

Sure, I did all of the terrible things I mentioned in *The Bipolar Advantage,* and followed every distraction I could find, but behind it all there was this deep desire to someday become the saint that I believed I should be. I always thought that I was just burning off desires and would sooner or later stop doing the things that didn't matter. Without those distractions, I would become the person that I really am. Looking back, I can see the foolishness in such a concept, but such is the power of delusion.

When I first went to the monastery, it felt like I had finally come home. For the first time in my life, it seemed that I was doing the right thing; I completely loved it. For the first year or so, it was the best time of my life; I was making so much spiritual progress that everyone looked to me as the example to aspire to - or so they thought. At that point in my life, I had the delusion to think that chasing after the highs associated with meditation was the essence of spiritual life. I had not yet discovered that true spiritual growth is to know who you really are and to change yourself into a better person.

It was during my life at the monastery that I had my first real depression. I was so exhausted that I could not work, show up for meditations, study, or even walk to the dining hall. I became confused, lethargic, and mostly just lay in bed all day. The doctors tested for low thyroid, but since my blood levels were fine, it remained a mystery until my mid forties. I was still very happy for a while, perhaps as a result of meditation, but my psychiatrist would say I was in what they call a "mixed state" - part depression and part mania at the same time.

Eventually, I was forced to leave when I became angry and started acting inappropriately. Devastated, I wandered hopelessly through life for a couple of years, before giving up all hope and returning to the wild life that I wrote about in *The Bipolar Advantage*. My behavior got increasingly worse as I wildly fluctuated between increasingly more extreme mania and depressions for the next 15 years.

In my late thirties, I found myself teaching Silicon Valley companies about internet technologies and helped start a new dot com company. That job had me traveling around the world and teaching so much that my bipolar condition was exaggerated to new extremes. I was going into rages five to ten times a day, although for unknown reasons, my depressions were not debilitating me. Perhaps it was the thrill of making $1,000,000 a year, but I doubt it. I was miserable and often joked that I had rented my soul to the devil.

After retiring at 42, I created a piece of software called *Introspection*, as a way to get back on the spiritual path. However, after a few months, the stock market crashed and depression set in like never before. It would fluctuate from a low grade feeling of unhappiness and lack of energy, all the way to suicidal. I would also occasionally go into mania, but without any of the associated happy feelings. Depression occurred about 70% of the time at that point in my life; it was often to such an extreme as to be unbearable, bordering on suicidal.

Life had no meaning and was not worth living. Even when I felt I had reached a state of true one pointed thought, the intended goal of meditation, I had no desire beyond ending my own life.

A byproduct of my deep depression was that I was beginning to go to the clinic regularly with symptoms of flu and other minor illnesses. Finally, the clinic said I had to see a doctor instead of just dropping in.

My first visit with the new doctor was a day I will never forget. After listening to my symptoms and looking over my history, he asked, "Did you ever consider that you might be depressed?" "No, I'm not depressed," I said, "I am just going through a lot of stress."

He asked if I knew the difference between stress and depression; I didn't. "Stress is the result of the things that happen to you. Depression is your inability to deal with the stress; it makes you unable to function normally. The reason you keep having physical problems is because you are depressed." This was a moment that changed my life forever. I finally began to realize that I was suffering from depression that I needed to address.

Although I was soon working with a professional therapist and getting medication from a psychiatrist, my depression was getting worse, while I was gaining control over my mania. I wrote in *The Bipolar Advantage* about how over the course of eight years (some of which was pre-diagnosis), I slowly turned rage around from five to ten times a day into my advantage. However, depression was still not completely addressed, because I had not been willing to face it. Denial is powerful, even in the face of overwhelming evidence.

It took almost five years before I realized that my behavior was the worst symptom of my condition. It is the way we act that affects everyone and makes our condition a terrible thing. Changing my actions became the central focus of my recovery, and I wrote the following as a way to hold myself to the task.

I Want To Be A Better Person

January 29, 2006

I have finally settled on a motto that says it all for me - I Want To Be A Better Person. For me, that simple phrase addresses many of my issues; my arrogance, my bad behavior, my admission of having done wrong, my acceptance of who I really am, and most of all, my need for hope. I Want To Be A Better Person reflects my belief that in spite of my bipolar condition, I can overcome my bad tendencies and become someone to admire, instead of someone to fear or feel sorry for.

My journey to wanting to be a better person was long and convoluted, painful, yet even funny at times. My hope is that by sharing it with you, I will have an even greater desire to live up to my dreams and give someone else hope as well. There are countless details left out and many details may be wrong, but I hope to paint a picture of how I got to this point.

Long before my diagnosis of Bipolar, I exhibited behaviors that were considered horrible, to put it mildly. Thinking I was smarter and better than anyone, I would justify my behavior as the fault of whoever was my victim. It was always "your" fault that I was acting so horribly, and if it weren't for you, I would be a saint. My extreme rages were outdone by my delusions, my denial that I was responsible for my behavior, or even believing that my behavior was perfectly justified.

After getting sick of my own behavior, I bought an estate that was next to the monastery that I once lived in. I volunteered to manage the computer systems department and was put under the direction of Lee, a senior monk who I have known for over 20 years. One day, I had a falling out with a friend of mine that I had hired to do some work for the monastery. We ended up in a heated email exchange that was rapidly escalating to the point that it was harming the monastery. Because I was representing the monastery, Lee insisted that all emails that I sent be approved by him. It has been almost five years now, but that experience is one that I have finally grasped.

Mike would send me an email that my deluded mind thought was rude. I wanted to reply with the full force of my rage, but knowing Lee would not approve it, I would rant and rave around the office until I calmed down enough to write the first draft.

I would read my draft to my co-workers and they would tell me, "There is no way Lee is going to let you say that." I would go for a walk, try to soak up some of the peace from the monastery, and go back for another try. My co-workers would again tell me "no way" and I would repeat the effort all day.

Finally, by the end of the day, or sometimes the next day, I would have a draft ready for Lee. He would calmly change what I had written into something that a saint would have written.

The process of receiving an email and taking all day to respond, went on for over a month. Towards the end, I told Lee that he was expecting me to act like a saint, to which he replied: "Did you expect anything less?"

A year or so later, I was diagnosed as being bipolar; I was back in form. I had quit my volunteering and went back to my old ways. Overtaken by delusions, I was sure everyone was out to get me. My preemptive strikes caused me to vent my rage at anyone I thought was a danger, literally everyone. The lesson Lee had tried to teach me had not only failed to sink in, I had never noticed it in the first place.

The diagnosis seemed like the worst thing that ever happened to me, but now I see it much differently. I finally saw that there was a reason for why I was acting inappropriately. As I resolved to get a handle on my "disorder," Lee stepped in again and tried to help me understand. He told me that it was not a "disorder," it was a "condition" that I had to overcome.

I put together a workshop so that I could gain the insight of other bipolar people. I decided to call it "Bipolar in Order" because I wanted to get the "disorder" under control.

Like most of what Lee tried to teach me, it has taken many years to understand what he meant by "condition." Does it really matter whether my actions are the result of a mental illness, or just the accumulation of bad habits? I don't think so. It is who I am today that matters. I finally realize what Lee was trying to help me understand. I now want to be a better person, and that desire makes me try to say and do the right thing, whether Lee is there to correct me or not.

Everything that happens to me — a post on a bulletin board that I do not agree with, an event that happens on the street or in a store, my daily interactions with my wife, my friends, and everyone I meet — creates the same process in me. My first thought is to go into a rage. I then think, "I want to be a better person" and try to temper my reaction. If I am doing well, I choose to not react right away and I think about how I would react if Lee was there. I sometimes even act in ways that would make him proud.

I am finding that my desire to do the worst is starting to go away. My ability to do the right thing, or at least something close to it, is getting stronger. Very slowly, I am becoming a better person. I don't beat myself up about it, but I do put a lot of thought into analyzing my efforts. My introspection is getting easier because I can honestly say that I have become a better person than six months ago.

It might sound simple, but putting it into practice is the hardest challenge I have ever faced. It is also the most rewarding. Some day I might even live up to Lee's hopes and become that saint.[1]

1 First published in Mental Health World, Vol. 4 Issue 3, p.8, Fall 2006, Editor, Karen Welch

The Art Of Seeing Depression

A year ago, I would have screamed in outrage if anyone had suggested that there is anything good about depression.

I struggled for many years with the incongruity in my belief that everything has both good and bad elements, even if we cannot find the good. War has brought about great societal change, natural disasters have sometimes resulted in new development, and movies have convinced us that killing the "bad guy" can be a good thing. But depression? I was convinced there was nothing good about depression: period. My struggle to find any good in depression seemed as hopeless as my despair while in it.

In my workshops, lectures, and communication with people who read *The Bipolar Advantage*, I was met with unanimous agreement that depression is truly all bad. My own depressions, getting deeper and more frequent as I grew older, were screaming at the idiocy of trying to find any good in the experiences. It seemed only a fool would look for any good in something so obviously devoid of even the smallest ray of light.

It took several years of deep introspection and contemplation to slowly come to grips with the possibility that I might find at least some ray of hope in depression. There had to be a lesson in it. At the least, my awareness and understanding of depression were increasing each time it happened, and with each new study I undertook.

So strong was my belief that I could find the Depression Advantage, that I became blind to the reality that at the time, the good was just not there. And then one day I found it! In an instant, my life changed drastically. I sat down, feverishly typing to capture the thought, and include it below as it was written at the time.

The Art of Seeing Depression

March 16, 2006

James Turrell is one of the most remarkable artists alive. He has an amazing understanding of light and perception. By using darkness and almost imperceptible light, his artwork totally changes the way we see the world. I think his work with light and darkness is a perfect metaphor for trying to see depression in a new light.

When you enter one of Jim's installations, it is so dark that you cannot see anything, or at least not much. The amount of available light is simply too little for our eyes to use. His artwork is not a picture on the wall; it is the entire environment, in which both the perception of the audience and time act as critical components.

If you stay long enough, your eyes begin to adjust to the lack of light. You start to see things that were there all along, but your eyes were not yet ready to perceive.

When you go back out into the "real" world, you bring an entirely new perspective; you begin to see everything in a whole new light (pun intended). Jim's work can truly be described as a discovery of the act of seeing.[1]

My own art is similar to Jim's in many ways. Like Jim, instead of using a brush to paint a picture, I choose to build an environment that blocks out light and helps me to perceive. Unlike Jim, my art is not in the physical world; it is in my interior world.

Instead of blocking out the physical light, I learn to block out the thoughts and feelings that distract me from seeing the more subtle light that shines within each of us. I then discover deeper truths hidden within my own consciousness. When I return to the external world, I begin to see the same subtle light in the eyes of everyone I meet.

My art is called meditation. I have been practicing it for over 45 years, sometimes as much as 8 hours a day. Meditation has given

---

1 Hatje Cantz, James Turrell, the other horizon, Exhibition catalogue. 2002 MAK, Vienna. p. 127

me the ability to "see" things in a much deeper way. It can be described as the discovery of the act of knowing.

I recently went through a fairly deep depression, and came out thinking a lot about James Turrell. I don't know if he is bipolar or experiences depression, but if he does, I bet he sees it in the way I do.

When I went into depression the first time, all I saw was darkness and pain. At the time, I thought it was unbearable, but looking back and comparing it to some of the far deeper hells I have since experienced, it was really nothing.

As my perception has grown, I am beginning to "see" things I never knew were there: good insights, lessons, and personal growth. In "seeing" clearly, I notice that now depression doesn't affect me so negatively. It now affects me much more, but in a positive way, at least according to the way I have learned to "see."

On a scale from one to five, I used to think of a five as experiencing no depression at all, and a one as so deeply depressed that I would attempt suicide. I thought four was a little painful, three even more, and two almost unbearable. Since there was no "light," and all I could "see" was pain, I judged my experiences solely on that basis.

As I spent more time trying to "see" in depression, I began to notice many things that were probably there all along, but I could not "look" through the pain to "see" them. As I started to discover the "act of seeing" in depression, I started to ponder the significance of my discoveries.

Each time I experienced depression, it became clearer to me. I began to redefine what depression was, based on the features that I could now "see" more clearly. My scale began to change, from a scale based on pain, to one based on a much richer perception of what was going on. I still define a five as "having no symptoms," and a one as "so difficult that I try to kill myself," but four, three, and two have become a rich and varied landscape.

I have also come to understand the significant difference between those who have "situational depression," caused by outward circumstances, and those who have what I consider "true depression," caused by mental illness. I have learned to articulate that clearly enough to make a difference in the lives of both those who are truly depressed and those who love and support them.

Everyone experiences some form of depression at least once in life. If it is really bad, it means extreme sadness, crying, inability to function fully, lethargy, dullness of thought, and more.

For most, it is caused by some great loss like the death of a loved one, or some other great tragedy.

You wake up in the morning so sad, you think you cannot get through the day. It might even debilitate you for a day or so, but for the most part, you get up, grab a cup of coffee, go to work, and somehow make it through the day, even if seriously diminished in your ability to perform. If it is really bad, this depression lasts for weeks or months, as you slowly get on with life. That is a three in my book. It is also about as deep as anyone gets from "situational depression," the kind that comes solely from outside circumstances and not from mental illness.

A two is not just the same thing with more intensity. It is fundamentally different than a three. In a two, the world becomes black and white. There is no color. There is an intense physical pain. Thoughts become confused. During such pain, I lose the ability to even remember a time when it was not like this. I can see no future when it might go away. (This is called "state specific memory" and is very common.) My mind keeps repeating "kill yourself, kill yourself, kill yourself," and I keep seeing visions of car crashes and every method of suicide that you can imagine. All I can do is hang on. A two is the worst kind of hell. (At the time of writing this, I erroneously assumed that a one meant you killed yourself from the pain of the two state.)

Being able to explain depression better and help others is great, but there is so much more. Central to my belief, is that nothing is all good or all bad, but a combination of good and bad components. We "see" the good and bad according to our ability to perceive and the filters that we place on ourselves, based on how we assign value. In my struggles with depression, I have been frustrated with my inability to "see" any good in it. In my recent depression and thoughts about James Turrell, I have begun to "see" depression in a whole new light. I am not ready to choose depression, but next time it comes, I look forward to exploring a whole new landscape.

I have noticed that aspects of depression that I used to consider a two and almost unbearable, I am now denoting as a three. I have also begun to gain tremendous insight into many things, including my spiritual life. It is from a spiritual perspective that I have really begun to see that depression can be a great thing. In my readings of the lives of saints, pain and despair is often mentioned as a catalyst that helped them to become better persons and act in a manner that is called saintly. After always struggling with this concept, I am now beginning to understand.

It was the misery of depression that brought me to the realization that I am mentally ill. The unbearable pain is what helped me to recognize the torture I have done to others. Without the heartache, I would never have learned who I really am, and come to understand the power of acceptance. Without the despair, I would not have had the desire to become a better person.

The saints talk about having a despair so strong it becomes unbearable. The despair they feel is specific, it is the agony they feel from not having a direct experience of God. The despair becomes so strong, that they would rather die than go another minute without Him. They describe it as getting to a point that their own sense of self becomes the thing that separates them from God; they feel that they "die" into oneness with the divine. I believe that is what Saint Paul meant when he said "I die daily."[1]

In my depressions, I feel tremendous despair. My mind keeps repeating over and over "kill yourself, kill yourself." What if my perception keeps becoming clearer and I start to notice that the despair truly is for God? What if the self that I am trying to kill, is the "little self" that is keeping me from realizing the true nature that I believe is in each of us. This is our divine self. Jesus said "The kingdom of God is

---

1 Bible, King James Version,1 Corinthians 15:31

within you.[1]" It seems that for at least some of us, it is depression and despair that gives us the ability to "see" our divine self. That is why depression is the best thing that ever happened to me.

It was two in the morning when I finished writing the above article, so I sent an email to Brahmachari Lee (my hero, as discussed in *The Bipolar Advantage*) and went to bed. First thing in the morning, I called Lee and went straight to visit him. It was with Lee that I realized the significance of the concept for me. Lee loved it. Five minutes into the conversation, I said something astounding, given my history: "We can sit around talking about how smart we are, or do what we should be doing - meditating."

In the almost 20 years since leaving the monastery, I had tried many times to meditate, but had never been able to go deep, or even keep up the simplest of meditation habits. It was somewhat of a miracle that I would suggest it at all.

We sat down to meditate and I instantly went into one of the deepest meditations of my life. There is a saying that when you put so much energy into creating the "milk" of peace in meditation, you should not spill the "milk" by going right into talking and joking. In my first step out of the chapel, the first words out of my mouth were "I don't know why everyone is afraid of spilling the 'milk'. It's all milk." Lee turned to my wife Ellen and said: "Tom's back," and we all laughed. It may sound silly, but the significance of that

---

1 Bible, King James Version, Luke 17:21

moment is the central theme of this book: even depression contains the "milk" of spiritual growth.

Please don't confuse the highs of meditation with spiritual progress. I believe our experiences in meditation have no meaning if they do not create changes in our daily lives. It is the realizations that I gained and the changes I made to my actions that really matter, not the highs produced by meditation.

In my workshops, I was beginning to ask people what they thought about the Depression Advantage. I was not getting a hostile reaction, so I knew I could explore it with others. After writing *The Art Of Seeing Depression* article, I began to more openly discuss it in my talks and workshops, as well as in my day-to-day conversations.

Is My Experience Valid?

Several months ago, I facilitated a workshop for 250 homeless people with mental illness. It went better than my expectations, but I did encounter some strong resistance from a few. As I was going through a "business plan" for mastering depression, I heard a comment that has been with me ever since - "It's easy for you. You are not homeless. You have no idea what it is like for us. Our struggle is so much harder just to stay alive, that we don't have the luxury of doing the work you are talking about..." It created questions in me that I have been thinking about ever since. What do I know? Is my experience somehow less than that of everyone else? Is my experience valid?

While it is true that my experience of homelessness was only for a brief period in my early twenties, I do think my experience of being bipolar is valid. I have over 40 years of direct personal experience of bipolar symptoms, often in extreme states. I have been facilitating workshops for the last five years, speak regularly to large audiences of both professionals and consumers, and am certified by the California Board of Behavioral Sciences to teach LCSW and MFT therapists[1]. I have lived introspectively, paying close

---

1 California Board of Behavioral Sciences PCE#4050

attention to my thoughts, feelings, and spiritual life. Since my immersion in this subject, I now have confidence that my personal experience of bipolar and depression is what gave me the most insight.

I find myself thinking along a similar line of reasoning when I hear someone who is not bipolar talk about his ideas. He portrays himself as an expert, while acting like I know nothing, since I don't have his degree. Unless you have experienced something directly, you only have a description of it. In the deepest sense, the only real understanding comes from direct personal experience. Of course, professional doctors and therapists have direct experience in dealing with patients, so their contribution is valid in those areas and very important to our success.

I hold beliefs about the bipolar condition that are very challenging to the "pervasive deficit-based view of people with psychiatric disorders that is held by both mental health professionals and the lay public alike," as so well said by Maureen Duffy, Ph.D. As a matter of fact, my view is the exact opposite – being bipolar is the best thing that ever happened to me. It was only my inability to deal with the condition that made me see it as an illness. Now that my condition is under my control, I see being bipolar as my greatest asset.

But maybe I don't suffer like everyone else. Maybe my condition is so slight that it was easy to control. Perhaps if my condition was half as bad as everyone else, I would see the folly in my thinking. To that end, I have been thinking long and hard about what my experience has been. I came to the conclusion that it is not the hardships we face that matter, it is what we become as a result of facing them.

Nonetheless, as there is no measurement to compare, the question remains - is my experience valid for someone else?

I have struggled the longest with coming to see depression as an advantage, although mania has just as many challenges, if not more. For me, and so many others I have met in talks and workshops, depression has four components: physical, mental, emotional and spiritual.

Each by itself can be unbearable at times, but combined, they have killed so many that there is great danger in encouraging someone to even go there. It is understandable that one would choose the boredom of an overmedicated life to the pain of depression.

While I don't see my own experience as that much different from others, I will talk about my last depression from all four components, and try to explain how it got me to seeing the bipolar condition as a great thing.

Physical Pain

Other than a broken ankle when I was 14, my physical body was fairly pain free until I experienced shingles[1] for the first time at 25. Shingles is often said to be the worst pain a man will ever experience. Women say child birth is worse, but shingles lasts much longer. My first episode continued over a month, and was so unbearable it was the only thing in my consciousness for the whole period. My shingles was spread across my chest and

---

1 "Shingles (herpes zoster) is an outbreak of rash or blisters on the skin that is caused by the same virus that causes chickenpox — the varicella-zoster virus."
http://www.ninds.nih.gov/disorders/shingles/shingles.htm

wrapped around my body like a band of pain. I have had it a few times since, but never as bad as the first time.

My last depression made shingles seem like nothing. The pain was just as bad, but it covered my entire body. Shingles is just at the surface of the skin, but my pain was everywhere, like a giant muscle cramp that would not go away. Some say 70% of people with depression have physical pain as part of it. Is that the pain they are talking about? I don't know. All I know is it was so painful that I stayed in bed for over a month as I could not move. With shingles to compare to the pain of depression, I believe I at least know my experience of the physical component of depression is valid.

There were times when the physical pain was so intense that it became the only thing in my consciousness. I write about this intensity in the chapter about Saint Teresa. Her pain was so far greater than I have ever experienced, and for so much more of her life, but I think I know what she means when she talks about getting to a state where she transcended the pain. There were times for me when the pain took me to a place where I felt a "peace which surpasses understanding."

Mental Pain

What is mental pain? How do you measure it? What goes on in one's mind that causes it? I only know what it is like for me. My mental pain is a combination of hallucinations, obsessive thoughts, thoughts of suicide, delusion, unclear thinking, and confusion—to name a few. My last depression consisted of mental pain at my all time worst, along with the physical pain I just related, plus the emotional and spiritual pains yet to be described.

I couldn't see. The bedroom was completely dark even in bright daylight. On the screen of darkness, I could see myself dying in many ways; driving into a gas pump and exploding, driving into oncoming traffic, jumping off a bridge, in front of a train, hanging, being cut into pieces, drowning, being beaten to death, every macabre scene you can imagine. The voices in my head kept shouting "Kill yourself, end it now, you are worthless, quit being such a burden, you are going to die right now." The voices went on and on. When I could think a thought other than death, it was paranoia and the possibility of being stuck in this state for eternity. It was eternity. Time seemed to just stand still.

Another mental pain that I share with many is what is called "state specific memory." While in a state of depression, I cannot remember a time when it wasn't like this. I can be reminded about a vacation we once took and remember it clearly, but only remember being depressed, even if I was not at the time. I also cannot envision a time when the depression will go away.

Is my experience valid? It is hard to compare mental pain because there is nothing physical to use as a reference. I do know, from talking to many others, that my experience is very common. The mind goes places we wish it never did, but we seem to have no control over it at times.

Emotional Pain

What is emotional pain? How is it different from mental pain? For me, mental pain is about thoughts, visions, and hearing, while emotional pain is more about feelings in the heart. I am one of those men who are not good at expressing emotions. Words like sadness, sorrow, dejection, misery, despondency, desolation, wretchedness, gloom, dolefulness, melancholy, mournfulness, woe, heartache, grief, and even despair can't convey the sheer pain I feel when all I can do is cry.

In some moments, there is nothing else but the emotional pain, which in a weird sort of way is a temporary relief from the physical and mental pain. It is there all along with the physical, mental and spiritual pain, but for brief periods, one of them becomes so overwhelming, I can't even notice the others.

Once again: Is my experience valid? Who knows? I may not be as good as some in describing it, but when others do, I know exactly what they mean.

Spiritual Pain

Why am I here? What is the point of life? Is there a connection to other people? Other beings? Is there a God? Have I lost all connection to everything? Does life have any meaning? Like the homeless man who claimed life was easy for me, I find myself thinking that those who talk about spiritual things have never lost the luxury of being able to ponder these questions.

When faced with the total annihilation of existence, the despair that accompanied my last depression was so deep that such questions were meaningless. Yet those same questions were central to the entire spiritual pain. At some point, there was just nothing. No me, no God, no life, no meaning, no connection, nothing. It was a true crisis of faith: a "Dark Night of the Soul," forty days in the desert, the loss of all purpose, all rolled up into a visit to hell without leaving the bed.

Some people like to talk about what it would be like to go to a place where nothing exists. Some even spend their lifetime meditating in an attempt to get there. I've been there and can tell you very clearly - it is the worst kind of hell. The physical, mental, and emotional pain were a pleasure compared to the despair of a total void. Life without meaning is no life at all.

Don't misunderstand, most people use meditation as a tool to find meaning; it is a powerful tool. Just be careful what your goal is. You might get there, and find out you picked the wrong one.

I wrote about my spiritual pain in *The Bipolar Advantage*. Some people misunderstood and were offended by what they perceived as attacks on their beliefs. I was, and still am, in a deep spiritual crisis. I know it seems illogical to express hostility to all things spiritual in one book and to include stories of saints in the next, but such is the nature of spiritual pain. While not claiming my experiences carry the validity of the saints, my own spiritual crisis is very real to me.

Is My Experience Valid?

Who knows? Maybe it never happened. Maybe the month in bed was just being lazy. Maybe there was no real pain, because my mind was just making it up. Maybe I'm just crazy. Perhaps I should have gone to the hospital, called my doctor, called 911. Do other people have legitimate pain? Am I making a mockery of it? That is the trouble with psychological pain. There is no cancer or broken leg to point at.

My doctor says it doesn't matter if I have suicidal thoughts; what matters is how I choose to act on them. Although in lesser depressions, it is entirely possible to attempt suicide, in the depths of my last one, it was not. It would have taken too much effort to even try.

In talking to many other bipolar people, I don't believe my experience is that different from most. We all get to states that can be called "hell." If there is any difference, it is in the way I reacted to it, but not in whether it was legitimate or not.

It is the nature of our condition to question ourselves about it. Self doubt is part of the mental pain and adds to the problem. The lack of any physical component, including no blood test or any other confirmation, only makes us more unsure of ourselves. In the final analysis, we must come to an acceptance that our condition is valid because of the concrete affects it has on our lives.

In one of my favorite books, *The Saints That Moved The World*, Rene Fulop-Miller talked about how modern psychologists (in the 1940s) would say that Saint Anthony's visions were all in his head. He concluded that it doesn't matter. What matters is what Saint Anthony became as a result of it.[1] In that regard, my physical, mental, emotional,

---

1 Fulop-Miller, Rene, *The Saints That Moved The World*, [New York] : T.Y. Crowell, 1945. pg 34

and spiritual pain is valid if it helps me to change myself into a better person.

Redefining Functionality

The primary goal of recovery is to increase functionality. Functionality is assumed to mean the ability to go back to work or find new work that is more compatible with the limitations imposed by the bipolar condition. The New Oxford American Dictionary, 2nd Edition[1] defines functionality as "the quality of being suited to serve a purpose well" or "the purpose that something is designed or expected to fulfill." Pretty clear definitions. How did they get changed into one limited to just work?

Any discussion of functionality in depression or the bipolar condition must include all aspects of life. Is the purpose of life to work, or is there more to life than just making a living? I'm not saying work is not a big part of life, just that things like getting along with others and personal growth are at least as important. The biggest reason we can't keep our jobs is that we have problems functioning in the social sense.

From the manic side, functionality actually increases at first in many bipolar people. In low level states, often called hypomania, we have more energy, less need for sleep,

---

1 New Oxford American Dictionary 2nd Edition, 2005, Oxford University Press, USA

increased mental function, greater creativity, and the ability to see relationships between concepts. As our level of mania increases, our ability to control the effects becomes impaired, and we eventually lose all control of ourselves. We become increasingly erratic, angry, delusional, impatient, etc. Those around us notice pressured speech, aggressiveness, and other symptoms that eventually escalate to a state where we become a danger to ourselves and others.

We are initially attractive to new employers because of our energy and enthusiasm. We are highly praised at work for our drive and ambition, and are often looked at as the best employees - until we begin to lose control. It doesn't take much time before we start exhibiting behaviors that make the management wish they never hired us in the first place.

When we get too manic, we start arguments with other workers and prove unable to function in groups. We begin to cause more trouble than we are worth. It is only a matter of time before our negatives outweigh the original positive impression that we gave. We can only hide our dark side for so long. No matter how productive we may be, the overall effect we have is to hurt the functionality of the whole organization.

The only thing worse than when we get too manic is when we get depressed. We don't get anything done and prove to be completely unreliable. We can't be counted on to finish our projects; sometimes we cannot function at all.

Is the problem our inability to keep a job, or is it something much more complicated than that? I think the bigger problem is that our definition of functionality is far too limited; we do not see the true picture. Functionality needs to be seen as state specific in both mania and depression. Our work aspirations need to change, to accommodate our new understanding of what is functional.

Functioning While Manic

The orthodox solution for mania is to keep it from happening, for fear that it will get out of control. But what if we could keep it in a range where we could still handle it? Through medication, therapy, personal insight, and determined effort, many people find that they can eventually enter hypomanic states and function just fine. Their increased ability to perform more than makes up for the negative parts. In some cases, their efforts to control themselves become strong enough that they are able to control the negatives and, at least for low levels of mania, are indeed enhanced by the condition.

When we see functionality in mania as more complex than just our ability to produce, we see that changing our behavior is the key to increasing functionality. If I were to accomplish many things, I would be considered productive. If I could produce more things than most people, one might even say I was "highly functional."

For example, if I could write a book in a week, people would consider this a major accomplishment. I did write a book in a week. But during that time I did not interact well with anyone. I barely ate, didn't sleep, ran my body ragged, and was impatient and crabby. In other words, I was highly functional in one part of my life, but dysfunctional in other important aspects. Yet by our society's standards, the book was a great accomplishment. By my definition, it was a great failure in functionality. True functionality must include all aspects of life, which in the manic side means being highly productive while also staying in control and acting better.

In the final analysis, acting better turns out to be more important than being productive, which is why mediocre people who know how to get along with others tend to be more successful than superstars who can't keep a job.

Learning to function in mania means to control your behavior via medication, therapy, and your own hard work. The only indication that we can function at any level of mania is how we act. If we can't keep our behavior under control, we are not functional; no matter how productive we think we are. Only when we prove that we can be at a certain level of mania while keeping our behavior under control, can we claim to be functional at that level.

The need to medicate so strongly that we are kept out of mania goes down over time. With the lower dose, the hypomania has a greater tendency to escalate, but with therapy, insight, and hard work, we can learn to function at the new dosage without the negatives creeping in. Is it possible to get to the point that we can function in higher manic states, while still controlling the negative effects? I believe it can be done, but it takes an effort much greater than most people are willing to make. I outline the steps in *How Do You Get There*, later in this book. This effort has rewards that redefine what it means to be fully functional. The ability to function in higher manic states without negative effects means enjoying the advantages offered from the bipolar condition without its adverse effects.

Functioning While Depressed

The lack of functionality in depression is an entirely different problem from the manic side of being bipolar. By the commonly mistaken definition of functionality, depression is the worst part of the condition. It seems clear to everyone that depression is a state of progressively decreased functionality to the point that "depression" and "lack of functionality" become almost synonymous.

The problem in depression is that our limited definition of functionality does not work at all. We need a definition that is specific to the state of depression and allows for functionality in areas outside normal measurements of productivity. The definition must take into account "the purpose that something is designed or expected to fulfill." Functionality in depression is not measured by how many things we can create.

Like those in lower levels of mania, many depressed people find that they can function in low levels of depression while controlling the negative effects. With the aid of medication, therapy, insight, and our own hard work, we lessen the negative aspects of depression while learning to gain from the experience. Eventually we get to the point where we can go deeper into depression without being overwhelmed by the pain, despair, delusion, and suicidal ideation.

As we learn to "see" in depression, we learn that depression can help us to produce changes in our lives. We become stronger. Our ability to empathize with and help others increases. We begin to gain perspective. We find that deeper states of depression start to lose their grip on us. Our ability to perceive becomes greater, and we notice a change in ourselves. We resolve to make changes in the way we treat other people. We develop a greater appreciation for simple things in life. We become better people.

As insights increase, we start to place a higher value on personal growth than on the accomplishment of things. We begin to see light in the darkness. Depression in these circumstances can be seen as highly functional and productive. During those times, depression gave me something far more valuable than a mere book. Depression gave me insight and the ability to change the way I see the world.

As with mania, the orthodox solution is to prevent depression from happening, for fear that it will get out of control. Both solutions deny the possibility that we can learn to be functional in these states. Living in fear is not functional either. Only by learning to function in both manic and depressed states can we achieve our real potential. As you will see in the chapters about the lives of saints, our potential is much greater than we are willing to admit. To achieve that, we need to recognize a higher purpose and learn to be more functional by changing the way we act in all circumstances. As I spoke about in *The Art Of Seeing Depression* article, the higher purpose of depression is to gain insight, learn what is really important in our lives, and find the will to change.

A New Definition

We can redefine functionality, once we have found the ability to accomplish great things WITHIN. My definition of functionality has become one based on personal growth above all other things. By that definition, depression is the most functional state I know. Every great change in my life was precipitated by insights gained during depression. Depression has served the function of changing my life for the better.

Increasing functionality means to learn to expand our ability to function in both manic and depressed states. Our natural ability to experience states outside the range of "normal" people can become the greatest gift. The gift comes with side effects originally beyond our control, but that does not mean that we cannot learn to function in higher states of mania and deeper states of depression. It is within our power to learn to control those states and turn them to our advantage.

The path is difficult and fraught with danger. It is much easier to just avoid anything outside of a narrow range. But how can you call that functioning, when so much more is available?

Getting Back To Work

Once we begin to understand what functionality means, and examine our good and bad traits, we can see that employment needs to be approached differently. Some jobs clearly will never work for us, but that does not mean that we cannot find work that is meaningful and rewarding. We just have to look for work that more closely matches our unique talents.

There are a ton of jobs that I am just plain incapable of keeping. I should know; I have burned through more than my fair share. I have also had several perfect jobs that would have lasted if I knew then what I know now. It may seem obvious, but we need to find work that fits our lives instead of trying to fit ourselves into jobs that we are not suited for.

Just like elsewhere in life, we have to take a hard look at what our good and bad traits are and come to an **acceptance** of them. We then need to **introspect** deeply to have a clear picture of what we are capable of. We need to **focus** on finding types of work that are appropriate, and **create a business plan** with the steps outlined on how to achieve it. We need to **get help** in whatever way we can, and do **our own hard work** to accomplish our goals. I outline these steps in the *How Do You Get There* chapter.

In following this process, you might find that you have pursued a career that was wrong for you all along. That is what Cathy discovered during one of my first workshops. In looking at the good and bad traits about bipolar that we all came up with, she realized that her career path was destined to fail from the start.

Cathy started and owned two businesses that did not give her satisfaction. She quit those, hoping that working for someone else would take away the burden that was causing too much stress and exacerbating her symptoms. When she attended the workshop, she was working as an accountant because of her training, but it was not fulfilling either.

All of her previous work had her sitting in a cubicle, with no external stimulus, interaction or travel. She came to realize that it was the boredom that was making her stressed, not the deadlines and challenges. Her jobs were increasing the amount of time that she had to cope with her weaknesses, and doing so increased mania and depression.

Seeing all the good and bad aspects of being bipolar made it all very clear. Cathy needed to accept her weaknesses and accept what wasn't working. Even if she was invested in her careers, she had to admit they weren't what she needed to be doing. Cathy also needed to accept her strengths: networking, easily understanding high level concepts, and making connections between distant people and situations.

Within months of the workshop, Cathy took a big gamble. She first found a new job, but then left the familiar and started on a career that was in line with her functionality. She has been at the same job now for almost four years, and finds it to be the most fulfilling job she has ever had. It not only challenges her through travel, networking, and dealing with high level concepts; it also affords her the ability to take time off when depression sets in.

Once you start working in an environment that supports your strengths and accommodates your weaknesses, life will begin to work for you too.

It is not always as easy as it was for Cathy. Sometimes we have to stay in a position that we hate just to keep food on the table. My work with homeless people taught me how some people struggle with all they have just to stay alive. But I never said it was easy. With determination, hard work, help, and some good luck, we can all eventually create a better living while changing ourselves into better people.

Redefining Our Scale

The Old Scale

    I mentioned in *The Art Of Seeing Depression* chapter that we often talk about where we are on a scale. I mentioned the bottom half of a scale that goes from one to 10, but did not bring up that there are no real standards. People like to compare it to a scale for physical pain, and mention how one person's 10 is another person's seven. The same thing happens with spicy food; I usually order a seven or eight out of 10, but sometimes it is deadly hot and other times fairly mild.

    The one to 10 scale is common among many support groups. When people check in and introduce themselves at a support group, or when they start a session with a doctor or therapist, they often indicate where they are on the scale. What I've learned from the workshops I've facilitated is that nobody really knows what this scale means.

    The one through 10 scale may be common among many support groups, but there is not much sense in it. First of all, a five is not even half way. There are five levels above and only four below. Worse yet, nobody seems to know the difference between a four and a two.

One possible solution is to change the scale to zero at the middle, with plus one through five for mania and minus one through five for depression. I think there are too many levels to differentiate, and prefer a scale of one through three. No matter which one you pick, the common misconception is that when you get to the deepest depression you will kill yourself, and when you get to the highest mania, everyone else will wish you were dead. :-)

Depression and bipolar are very deadly. Forty percent of us sooner or later attempt suicide; 20 percent of us succeed. Some people attempt suicide when they get to minus two, others when they get to minus one. There isn't an exact place on the scale where it happens. It is different for every individual. We can't assume that we know where on the scale any individual will be when a suicide attempt is made.

On the upper end of the scale, the common belief is that the further up we get, the less rational we become, and the more we start acting in a way that endangers ourselves and others.

The common conception is that the pain of depression is just progressively worse as you go down through four, three, two, and finally one, where you are at the greatest risk of suicide.

Out of fear that we will flip out and kill ourselves, we think that we need to stay at zero all the time. We can use drugs and therapy to keep us there, but we become bored. As far as we are concerned, we might as well be dead. We stop taking our medicine and end up flipping out, just as we feared.

Dead
+3
+2
+1
0
-1
-2
-3
Dead

Bored

Drugs & Therapy

Target Zone

The real problem is that we are trying to live an existence that has no ups or downs. If forced into a life that is boring, we are not going to stay on the program. It is not a life worth living. Staying at zero is not functional and will never satisfy us in the long run.

Another problem with the scale is that it has minus for depression and plus for mania. Why would we say mania is a plus? The reason that some people say mania is a plus, is they have never had to put up with someone who is out of control. Those of us who have been manic, or have had to put up with a manic person, know it can be a minus every bit as bad as depression.

Although the "thermometer-based" scale accounts for calling someone a hothead, it does not account for mixed states. In the context of bipolar disorder, a mixed state is a condition during which symptoms of mania and depression occur simultaneously: "for example, agitation, anxiety, aggressiveness or belligerence, confusion, fatigue, impulsiveness, insomnia, irritability, morbid and/or suicidal ideation, panic, paranoia, persecutory delusions, pressured speech, racing thoughts, restlessness, and rage all at the same time."[1]

-3

-2

-1

0

-1

-2

-3

To accommodate mixed states and the concepts I am going to build in this chapter, the chart ought to look more like the one below:

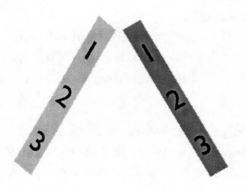

1 http://en.wikipedia.org/wiki/Bipolar_disorder#Mixed_state

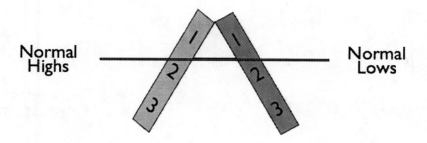

The New Scale

Everyone has normal highs and lows. At times, they can be perceived as a minus even for normal people. Many times, the actual characteristics are those of a mixed state, a little depressed and agitated at the same time. Our new scale accommodates the negatives associated with any normal range of experience. Those with bipolar or depression live in fear of these normal highs and lows, but without the range of experiences that fit in area 1 on the chart, life is not worth living.

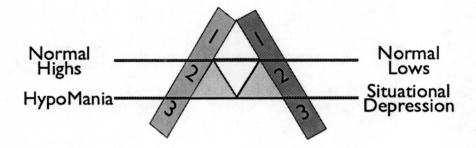

At least once in life, everyone will experience the range of mood in the two area. It includes hypomania and situational depression. Mild hypomania is felt when we cram for an exam, or are so excited about tomorrow that we can't sleep. Situational depression is when something happens to us that causes us pain.

Situational depression is usually caused by the loss of a loved one or something that has meaning, but can be triggered by any event. When we get to that level, the details are consistent for almost everyone. We should open our eyes and try to understand it. It is the same for so many people that we can all describe it clearly, as I did in *The Art of Seeing Depression* chapter.

If you view the white areas as the range of "normal" people, it illustrates that they experience the more extreme states less often, and for a finite length of time. Bipolar and depressed people get there all the time. Sometimes, it is just the beginning of a slide into clinical depression or mania.

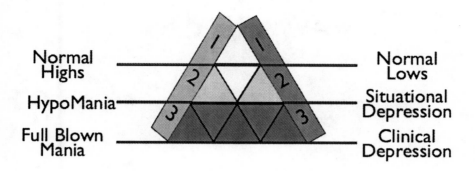

Normal Highs — Normal Lows
HypoMania — Situational Depression
Full Blown Mania — Clinical Depression

There is another state that "normal" people never experience or fully understand. This other state includes clinical depression and real mania. Area three is for those extreme states.

It is so much more extreme, that people who have only experienced situational depression have no idea what it is like. As explained in *The Art of Seeing Depression* chapter, this is not a matter of degree, it is a difference in kind.

There are very clear, and very painful aspects to clinical depression. It has four components: physical, mental, emotional, and spiritual. They are described in the chapter *Is My Experience Valid?* and in the following chapters on the lives of the saints.

It is unfortunate that so many people with clinical depression have to experience this state with so little real understanding.

AWARENESS

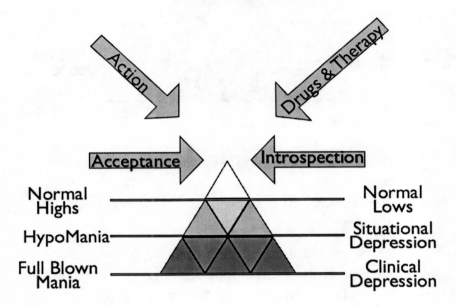

We begin to gain control when we start on a program of drugs and therapy. The drugs calm us down in a major way. They help us to find a range we can function in. Unfortunately, some doctors over-medicate and we are stuck at zero where life is not worth living. But that isn't the goal. The goal is to stop the worst of it from happening.

Therapy helps us reach a point called **Acceptance**. Until we accept our condition, there is nothing we can do; we are in denial. Some people say, "There's nothing wrong with me. I don't need medication. I'm going to take care of it myself. I've got it all handled." That is delusion. It is an attitude that will not get you anywhere. Acceptance is the first step we must take before we can make any progress.

Our therapists and clergy help us to begin **Introspection**. As we pay closer attention to our thoughts, actions, and spiritual lives, we start to understand what is happening.

Once we begin to see ourselves the way others see us, we realize that we can take **Action**; there are very concrete things that we can do to change ourselves. We can take our medication, follow the advice of our therapists, change our diet, exercise, adjust our sleep patterns, and do all kinds of things that will help us to gain control. I outline some of them later in this book. Once we take action, we find it is easier to stay in control with lower dosages of medication and less dependence on therapy.

At first, I had to go to the doctor every day and take massive doses of lithium. It wasn't long before I only went once a week, then once a month, and finally, once every few months. Now, I see therapy and drugs as a small part of my program. I'm also taking action.

We eventually develop **Awareness** of how we react to things and the choices that we can make. This leads directly to stability because we have less fear and less panic about staying in a narrow range. This is the beginning of realizing what the *Depression Advantage* is all about.

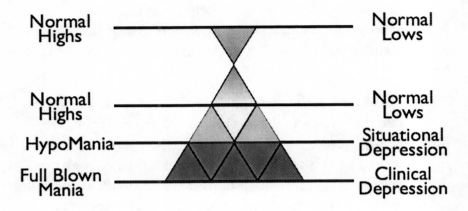

When we come to awareness, we understand what's going on, and everything changes. We start to realize that everyone goes into normal highs and lows, and they are not necessarily all bad. Yes, highs and lows have their bad points, but they also have their good points. A mature view of the normal experience of life is that nothing is all bad or all good. It's a combination: there are good things to learn even from our low points. They make us stronger, inspire us to introspect, and help us realize what has meaning to us.

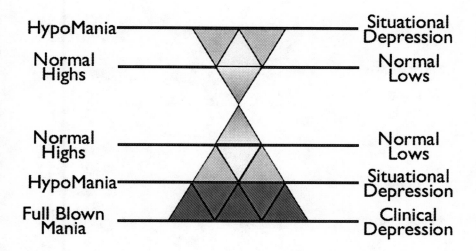

The same can be said for hypomania and situational depression. It seems at first that getting into a situational depression is nothing but horrible. However, if you introspect enough, and you actually start looking for it, you see that great good can come from even our worst experiences.

We are able to help other people. We are able to understand other people's circumstances; We empathize better. Going through those experiences ourselves makes us stronger and better people, once we see how to learn from them. It is possible for everyone who has these experiences to see them for what they are: a combination of good and bad. Those of us with mental conditions have more opportunities to learn from our experiences and grow to become better people.

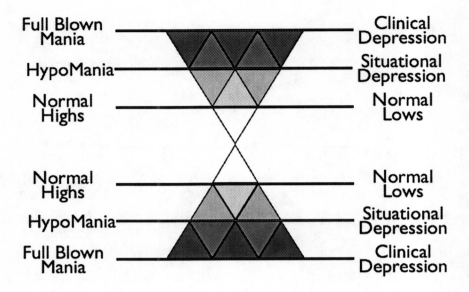

Full Blown Mania		Clinical Depression
HypoMania		Situational Depression
Normal Highs		Normal Lows

Normal Highs		Normal Lows
HypoMania		Situational Depression
Full Blown Mania		Clinical Depression

In a book called *The Depression Advantage*, one might hope that this page would include an easy answer. We explored the negatives of all the stages and came up with reasonable approaches to the easy stuff, but this is where the challenge is. How can anyone see an advantage to the worst states?

I've been to the hell of clinical depression many times and could not see any good in it. Just like on the negative side, the intensity of clinical depression is such that those who have not been there may never fully understand. As I mentioned in *The Art of Seeing Depression* chapter, we have to change our way of "seeing" to begin to notice what has been there all along.

When I started looking at it like James Turrell would, and tried to see in that darkness, I started realizing that it wasn't all pain. There are insights that I could have only learned by being there. Those insights are at the core of *The Depression Advantage*.

To everyone else, changing our behavior is the only thing that matters. Depression and pain are the strongest catalysts there are for creating behavioral change. They have helped me to fundamentally change the way I treat other people.

As you read about the lives of saints later in this book, you will find that I am not alone in my belief. Many saints have said that it was the intensity of extreme pain that helped them to see everything differently. They too credit pain with causing their behavioral changes.

A New Paradigm

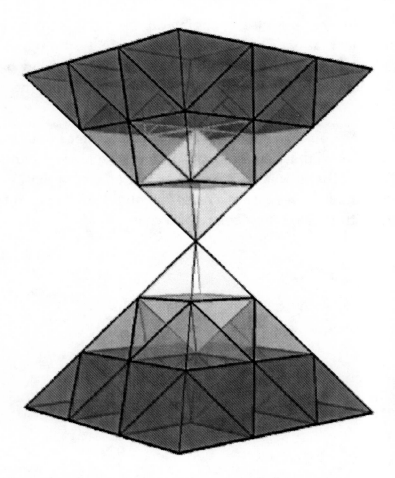

The old paradigm of mental illness will never get us
to the advantage. Looking at only the negative side of
anything will never give you the real picture. When seeing
your condition from only the negative, it is understandable
how you could conclude that life is hopeless, and settle for a
diminished life. The paradigm is not only false, it affects

everything you do and keeps you from ever leading a better life.

The new paradigm is about seeing the whole picture. Only by looking at both the bad and good of our condition, can we see what is possible. There is no denying that the bipolar or depressive condition has horrible down sides, but until you accept the possibility of seeing the good, you are condemned to a hell with no possibility of parole.

It is a four sided thing we're talking about. There are physical, mental, emotional, and spiritual components. It is a much more complex picture than most people would believe. When we start to see the complexity of it, we start to realize that the life of a normal person is missing a lot of opportunities. Is it a bad or a good thing that we have depression? It depends on how we react to it.

Although I have been familiar with the lives of many saints for a long time, it was not until I started to see the good in depression that I saw how it was central to the lives of so many of them. I began to realize that Saint Francis and Saint Theresa talked about the same things. Saint John of the Cross wrote a book called *The Dark Night of the Soul*[1] about how depression is a path to enlightenment. The painful times in their lives changed them fundamentally.

Saint Francis hung out with his friends, partying all night. When he faced depression, there was something about it that fundamentally changed his life. He became a person who people revere and an example we should all strive to follow.

---

1 The Dark Night of the Soul, translated by E. Allison Peers, 1990 Random House, New York

What is it that made his experience a transformation, yet does not have the same effect on all of us? It's not that he was born that way. He chose to look at his experience and find profound meaning in it. Why can't we? If that is possible, don't we have the opportunity to grow from our experiences? Is there something from these experiences that we can learn from? Is it all bad? Or, is there the possibility that we can learn something that has real meaning and can make a difference in our lives?

It is not the situations that make us who we are; it is how we choose to react to those situations. Saints became saints because of the way they reacted to the challenges in their lives. They kept trying to change, learn, and improve.

I think mental conditions - and personally, I refuse to call them an illness anymore - have the opportunity to teach us things that other people will never experience. It is the best opportunity of our lives. It is so rich, that when I look at my opportunities to live in that world, versus the narrowly defined world of a so-called "normal" person, I choose the hardships of my life every time. Yes, it has its hells, but it also has its heavens.

Saints Are People Too

I seem to be one of the few people who uses the word "saint" other than in the name of a church down the street or a city named for a saint to which it has long since lost any connection. The idea that it is possible to become a saint is so utterly preposterous as to enrage many people for the sheer mention of it.

The New Oxford American English Dictionary, 2nd Edition defines a saint as "a person acknowledged as holy or virtuous and typically regarded as being in heaven after death."[1]

Wikipedia has an interesting page about saints and even talks about the concept of sainthood being common to nearly all religions.[2] My studies of various religions confirm this idea: all faiths look up to those who rise above their circumstances and choose to act in a more perfect manner.

Krishna said: "out of a thousand people, one wants to know me. Out of a thousand who wants to know me, one

---

1 New Oxford American Dictionary, 2nd Edition ,2005, Oxford University Press, USA

2 http://en.wikipedia.org/wiki/Saint

actually does.[1]" In the context of the *Bhagavad Gita*[2], what he meant is that one person out of a million actually realizes the potential in all of us to become a saint. I personally find it very encouraging that one in a million can become saints. The common conception is that it is impossible except for the rare few in every century. With the current world population at 6.5 billion[3] that makes 6,500 saints walking around today, 36 of them in California.[4] My odds of becoming a saint are almost as good as my odds of becoming a congressman.

It all depends on what you call a saint. The classic definition is a person who is admired or venerated because of their virtue. Others say a saint is someone who has a personal contact with God. Although I agree with the mystical component, I think the primary qualification of a saint is to act like one.

Having studied the lives of saints for many years, it is the possibility that I may someday act like a saint that motivates me to become a better person. In my foolish pursuit of the "high" associated with alleged contact with God, I completely missed the point. It is not the feelings one gets in meditation that makes one a saint, it is the feelings other people get in one's presence that matters. That feeling is most often a result of acting "saintly" by choosing to act in the best way possible for every given circumstance.

---

1 Bhagavad Gita, Chapter VII, verse 3, translated by Parahmahansa Yogananda. 1995, Self Realization Fellowship, Los Angeles

2 Bhagavad Gita, translated by Parahmahansa Yogananda. 1995, Self Realization Fellowship, Los Angeles

3 http://en.wikipedia.org/wiki/Population

4 http://quickfacts.census.gov/qfd/states/06000.html

A Saint Is A Sinner
Who Never Gave Up[1]

One of the most overlooked aspects of the saints is that they were not born that way. The great thing about saints is the example they set; one that anyone can achieve. Many saints did things that would shame a bipolar, yet at some point in their lives were able to transcend their tendencies and change themselves.

In the two years since writing *The Bipolar Advantage*, I have been through some remarkable changes. I have had more spiritual growth in the last year than all of the previous years combined. I believe it is a direct result of admitting my flaws and using introspection to find a better way to act. I used to pursue the experience of peace through meditation and contemplation alone, but I now find that acting properly gives me a "peace which surpasses all understanding."[2] I am not the same man who I was even a year ago. I am beginning to become someone that I can be proud of, and hopefully will continue on a path of improvement for the rest of my life. Maybe some day I will be able to act "saintly" all of the time and inspire others to try to act the same.

Another overlooked aspect of sainthood is that they weren't necessarily perfect in all ways. Saint Joan of Arc was probably bipolar. If you wonder what rage looks like, look no further than the story of Joan of Arc.[3] She was out of

---

1 Sayings of Paramahansa Yogananda, 1980 Self Realization Fellowship, Los Angeles, p. 6

2 Bible, World English Bible, Philippians 4:7

3 Twain, Mark, Joan of Arc, 1989 Ignatius Press, San Francisco

control in so many ways, yet somehow inspired her whole nation. Although Joan also showed signs of depression, I chose others for this book because her example is mostly about the manic side.

As you read the lives of the saints in this book, I hope you notice that their lives were not perfect either. Each of the saints were endowed with traits we should admire along with struggles to improve themselves that lasted to the end of their lives.

The point is, being a saint is possible for each and every one of us. The beauty of the concept of sainthood is that it is something we can all achieve, no matter what our past or current circumstances. For many, our greatest flaws can be turned into the path to sainthood. The real path to sainthood is in recognizing who we really are and determining to change those aspects of ourselves that keep us less than what we can be.

The lives of those who have followed the path to sainthood can be a great inspiration and guide for our own journey. In my struggles to find anything good about depression, it was the examples set by many saints that made me "see the light" that even depression can be seen as an advantage. The stories of their lives can be the stories of our own.

In choosing who to describe in this book, I was amazed to find that there are so many saints across every religion who had depression. My choices were based on my familiarity with them and how they would illustrate each aspect of depression - physical, mental, emotional and spiritual. Even more amazing is how depression was more than just a part of their lives - it was a big factor in their conversion from mere mortal to a life to revere. I hope that in reading their life stories, you will be inspired to change your own life into a story that inspires others.

Teresa of Avila

Sometimes I would suffer so many bitter spiritual trials, compounded by such severe bodily pain and sickness that I was left utterly helpless. This still happens even now, although to a lesser degree. At other times, I grew seriously ill, but since I was not experiencing that soul suffering, I bore it with great joy. It was only when all my afflictions were combined that I was reduced to such a miserable state.[1]

St. Teresa of Avila

Physical Pain Was Her Catalyst

If we are looking for examples of people who specifically overcame physical pain and transformed their lives through it, then Teresa of Avila is our saint. Not just because she had pain, but because it was severe and persistent throughout her life, and seemed to be a key to her enlightenment and elevated states of consciousness: what she called "union with God."

---

1 Teresa of Avila, translated by Mirabai Starr, The Book of My Life, New Seeds Books, Boston, 2007 p. 231

A life of prayer, meditation, and contemplation were very important to Teresa. Her most important work, the spiritual classic *The Interior Castle*, outlines the seven states of prayer and contemplation leading to "union with God." There can be no doubt that Teresa followed every method the church offered her: she introspected deeply and lived the life she espoused in her teachings and convents.

What is remarkable is the way she faced unbearable pain and chose to see it as part of her path to God. Rather than resisting it, she accepted it, and was eventually elevated by it. Pain turned out to be the vehicle and the catalyst to her ultimate realizations. Physical pain became a central part of her spiritual path.

"There is something universally appealing about Teresa of Avila," writes Mirabai Starr. "I can think of no other saint of the Catholic Church, except for Francis of Assisi, who so easily transcends the boundaries of institutionalized religion and reaches directly into the heart of the human experience... Her deep compassion for the suffering of humanity, grounded in her own experience of physical pain and emotional anguish, combined with a warm sense of humor and earthy practicality, made her accessible, comforting, and inspiring."[1]

Sixteenth Century Spain

Very close to the time that Teresa was born, the Catholic Church had started its world wide Reformation in response to the Protestants.

---

1 Interview with Mirabai Starr Library Journal, "Spiritual Living" Column, Jan 1, 2007

In Spain, a political war was raging under the guise of the Reformation. In 1492, King Ferdinand II of Aragon had pressured the pope to let him set up an Inquisition. While originally a war to remove the Muslims and Jews from Spain, in the 16th Century, the Inquisition also began targeting Protestants, heretics, witches and others.[1] During this time, any deviation from the orthodox religious experience came under strict observation and scrutiny. Any hint of thought or activity that did not closely adhere to the Church's laws was immediately suspected to be heresy.

Devotion was promoted as the correct path, because it relied on practiced rituals and not original philosophy or individual interpretation. Mystics were scrutinized because anyone who was in direct contact with God might undermine the authority of the Church. Only Church officials could speak with God directly.

The reign of Pope Paul IV (1555-1559), was determined to eradicate Protestantism and renew the church. Two of his key strategies were the Inquisition and censorship of prohibited books. In this sense, his aggressive and autocratic efforts of renewal greatly reflected the strategies of earlier reform movements - burning heretics and strict emphasis on Canon law.[2]

This atmosphere of persecution characterized the sixteenth century that Teresa would live and work in. While Teresa of Avila was eventually counted among the great reformers like Saint Francis, Saint John of the Cross, and

---

1 http://en.wikipedia.org/wiki/Spanish_Inquisition

2 Perez, Joseph, The Spanish Inquisition: A History, trans. by Janet Lloyd, 2005, Yale University Press, p. 45-52

Saint Philip Neri, she walked a difficult path in an age of fear and suspicion.

Early Childhood

Teresa was born in 1515 and had a comfortable childhood, growing up in a devoutly Catholic home. She also had a sense of adventure and a desire for spiritual life. When Teresa was seven years old, she attempted to run off with her brother to become martyrs in Africa:[1]

"One of my brothers was nearly of my own age; and it was he whom I most loved, though I was very fond of them all, and they of me. He and I used to read Lives of Saints together. When I read of martyrdom undergone by the Saints for the love of God, it struck me that the vision of God was very cheaply purchased; and I had a great desire to die a martyr's death - not out of any love of Him of which I was conscious, but that I might most quickly attain to the fruition of those great joys of which I read that they were reserved in Heaven; and I used to discuss with my brother how we could become martyrs. We settled to go together to the country of the Moors, begging our way for the love of God, that we might be there beheaded."[2]

This story ends with Teresa's uncle finding them on the streets of Avila, and returning them home to their parents. It illustrates the romanticism and spiritual nature of her upbringing. Her father read to her the lives of saints, and her mother introduced her to romantic tales of knights in

---

1 http://www.stthomasirondequoit.com/SaintsAlive/id743.htm

2 The Life of St. Teresa of Jesus, Teresa of Avila, trans. by David Lewis, 2006 BiblioBazaar, NY, p.70

foreign countries. As a young girl, she was devotional, prepared to renounce the world and live the life of a saint. She was also an adventurous romantic with a flare for the dramatic.

Early spiritual aspirations

Teresa's memories and impressions of her youth are recorded in *My Life*.[1] She said that her parents were good, pure, and devout. As a young girl, she would play in the orchards, build imaginary convents, and pretend to live as a hermit. These were her childhood imaginings - probably based on what she had learned about the lives of saints. Her reflections on her childhood are that God had arranged everything perfectly for her, so that she would be able to enter her spiritual vocation.

Her own account is that she was too giddy and careless to be trusted at home after her mother died. When Teresa was 16, her family decided she should attend school at the convent of St. Augustine. She entered the convent school and stayed a year and a half.

All the while, God was calling her. She was not willing to listen to His voice; she would ask the nuns to pray for her that she might have light to see her way; "but for all this," she writes, "I wished not to be a nun."

Teresa's stay at the convent was cut short because she began experiencing for the first time the symptoms of illness and pain that would only increase throughout her life. Since the source of her illness could not be diagnosed, and the

---

1 Teresa of Avila, The Book of My Life, trans. by Mirabai Starr, 2007 Shambhala Publications, New Seeds.

symptoms were misunderstood, she had to return home to her father.

"Among the many unusual experiences mystics have recorded, one of the most enigmatic is a peculiar type of traumatic physical seizure often accompanied by powerful, disruptive emotions. Teresa of Avila seemed particularly prone to these disturbances... So frequent were these attacks and so intimate a part of her mystical path that they have come to be regarded as one of the hallmarks of Teresa's spirituality."[1]

Becoming A Nun

Teresa was very attracted to the vocation of a religious life, but she also questioned herself constantly. Was she trying to get off easily for her sins? Did she think if she spent her life at the convent she could avoid purgatory and go straight to heaven? Would becoming a nun save her from her own bad judgment and actions? She admits in her writings to being very attracted to the sweet rewards of heaven and wanting to take the quickest path to get there.

Teresa had an uncle that was very devout and who lived an almost monastic life at his home in his later years. She once stayed with him for three days, and that visit seems to have had a lasting impression. The letters of St. Jerome, which she read there, filled her with courage. After reading the letters, she resolved that she would become a nun.

This was not a decision that had come easily; she was still unsure of herself. When she told her father of her

---

1 A Reappraisal of Teresa of Avila's Supposed Hysteria, Christopher M. Bache, Ph.D., Journal of Religion and Health, Vol.24, No.4, Winter 1985

decision to become a nun, she knew she would not go back on her word.[1] Her father did not want her to go, and forbade her to join the convent at this time.

There was no way she could persuade him; he would not listen to those whom Teresa had asked to speak to him on her behalf. She kept her resolve and left her home. Teresa secretly joined the Carmelite convent of the Incarnation, located just beyond the village of Avila. She was 20 years old.

"I remember... while I was going out of my father's house - the sharpness of sense will not be greater, I believe, in the very instant of agony of my death," she wrote years later. "It seemed as if all the bones in my body were wrenched asunder... There was no such love of God in me then as was able to quench the love I felt for my father and my friends."[2]

When she first entered the life of the convent, she had states of prayer so high that she was alarmed by them. She was so humble that she could not believe graces so great could be given to a beginner like herself. Few believed that this romantic and spirited novice deserved the mystical experiences she was beginning to have at the convent.

Teresa was overcome by unexplained emotional and devotional experiences from the very beginning. She was having visions and hearing voices. Because of the culture of the Reformation, many of her peers tended to believe that these were delusions influenced by "evil" or the "devil." As

1 The Life of St. Teresa of Jesus, Teresa of Avila, trans. by David Lewis, 2006 BiblioBazaar, NY, p.82

2 Teresa of Avila, translated by Mirabai Starr, The Book of My Life, New Seeds Books, Boston, 2007 p. 7.

a result, Teresa lost the confidence to continue her prayers and her spiritual life was almost put on hold. Even though she was living at the convent, she was not even practicing her meditations any more.

Teresa's Physical Pain

As soon as Teresa got back on the path, her progress was stalled by severe physical illness. In 1538, she was sent to the convent in Becedas to try to cure her. They had mineral hot springs that they hoped would alleviate her condition.

"I remained three months in that place, in the most grievous sufferings; for the treatment was too severe for my constitution. In two months - so strong were the medicines - my life was nearly worn out; and the severity of the pain in the heart, for the cure of which I was there was much more keen: it seemed to me, now and then, as if it had been seized by sharp teeth. So great was the torment, that it was feared it might end in madness. There was a great loss of strength, for I could eat nothing whatever, only drink. I had a great loathing for food, and a fever that never left me. I was so reduced, for they had given me purgatives daily for nearly a month, and so parched up, that my sinews began to shrink. The pains I had were unendurable, and I was overwhelmed in a most deep sadness, so that I had no rest either night or day."[1]

When that did not work, they sent her home to her father's house for about two years. Some believed it was malaria; but that didn't explain why she would experience

---

1 The Life of St. Teresa of Jesus, Teresa of Avila, trans. by David Lewis, 2006 BiblioBazaar, NY, p.96-97

this pain for a lifetime. At one point, it was so severe that she lapsed into a coma for four days. No one believed she would recover. She was returned to the convent, but remained paralyzed for three more years.[1]

"The pain is so excessive that one can hardly bear it, my pulses almost cease to beat, my bones are all disjointed, and my hands are so stiff that sometimes I cannot clasp them together. Until the next day I have pains in the wrist, and in the entire body, as though my bones had been wrenched asunder."[2]

"During the time that it lasts we cannot think of anything that has to do with our own existence: it instantaneously enchains the faculties in such a way that they have no freedom to do anything, except what will increase this pain. I should not like this to sound exaggerated: in reality I am beginning to see, as I go on, that all I say falls short of the truth, which is indescribable."[3]

As the episodes continued, Teresa began to understand them better. She was a close observer of her own mental states and her spiritual experiences. She began to recognize that she could simultaneously experience divine joy and an inner sense of peace during episodes of intense physical pain of the body.[4] The pain was intimately bound to

1 Teresa of Avila: Mystical Writings, ed. Tessa Bielecki, 1999,Crossword Publishing Company, NY. p. 200

2 Teresa of Avila: The Life of Teresa of Jesus (1565). Trans. and ed. by E. Allison Peers. New York, Image Books, 1960, pg.195.

3 http://www.catholicfirst.com/thefaith/catholicclassics/stteresa/castle/interiorcastle4.cfm

4 http://www.biographyonline.net/spiritual/st_teresa_avila.html

her spiritual progress. It was part of her direct "divine" experiences.

Teresa showed great courage when she continued on her path and her commitment to be a nun. She began her vocation in physical pain and self doubt. It could not have been easy to persevere. In the life of the convent, she did her best not to attract attention to herself or her own suffering.

"Teresa teaches us that poor health is not an obstacle to spiritual growth but actually enhances it. Why? We learn patience and surrender. We learn how to transcend the body and rise above both sickness and health altogether."[1]

These first years in the convent were just the beginning of a life that completely excavated the territory of prayer, devotion, meditation, life work, pain, persecution, mystical experience, and her ultimate goal, "union with God." Teresa spoke often of the lack of separation between these aspects of her life. In this sense, it was "all milk."

Teresa Founds Her First Convent

At the age of 43, Teresa decided she wanted to start a new order, recommitting to the values of poverty and simplicity. She wanted to move away from her present convent which had a very social atmosphere and made a life of prayer more difficult. Initially, her aims were greeted with widespread opposition from within the town of Avila. However, the opposition waned and she was allowed to set up her first, very modest convent. She guided the nuns not

---

1 Teresa of Avila: Mystical Writings, ed. Tessa Bielecki, 1999, Crossword Publishing Company, NY. p.111-112

just through strict disciplines, but also through the power of love and common sense.[1]

In 1567, she received permission to establish new houses of her order. Between 1567 and 1571, she opened several convents. In this effort, she made long journeys through nearly all the provinces of Spain. She was an energetic and powerful administrator, and a strong and compassionate spiritual advisor. She accomplished all of this while suffering from various illnesses and pain almost daily.[2]

Teresa Meets John Of The Cross

After receiving permission to establish monasteries for men, Teresa went in search of someone she could rely on for that job. She would need an energetic, educated, and devoted ally in this project. She met John of the Cross in 1567. Teresa highly regarded John's skill as a director. They would end up spending years working together to establish convents and monasteries for the contemplative life. As revered spiritual guides for the Reformed Carmelite nuns and fathers, each supported the other tremendously on the spiritual path. Their friendship and alliance remains legendary.

Teresa was 27 years John's senior, an experienced mystic, and already an accomplished author on the spiritual life.[3] She was determined to reach her goal of "union with God" and relied on her intimate, spiritual conversations

---

1 http://www.biographyonline.net/spiritual/st_teresa_avila.html

2 http://en.wikipedia.org/wiki/Teresa_of_Avila

3 http://carmelitesofeldridge.org/juan2.html

with this young priest to help her understand her own experiences.

John guided Teresa during the years when she reached the height of her spiritual life. In 1572, while receiving Communion from the hands of John of the Cross, she had a complete, mystical "union with God." Forever after, she regarded him as "the father of my soul."[1]

To understand the role Teresa's physical pain contributed to this moment, we need only turn to her own writings to see that this all encompassing sensation left her no option but to surrender to the spirit. Through the intense laser of pain, she focused on the "peace which surpasses all understanding,"[2] and achieved her "union with God" by leaving all thought of self, the body, and its senses behind.

"It sometimes happens that, when a person is in this state of great pain, and has such yearnings to die, because the pain is more than she can bear, that her soul seems to be on the very point of leaving the body... Relief comes as a general rule, by a deep rapture or some kind of vision... it produces the most wonderful effects and the soul at once loses its fear of any trials which may befall it."[3]

"And what a tremendous reward; one moment is enough to repay all the trials that can be suffered in a life!"[4]

---

1 The Life of St. Teresa of Jesus, Teresa of Avila, trans. by David Lewis, 2006 BiblioBazaar, NY, p.486-87

2 Bible, World English Bible, Philippians 4:7

3 Interior Castle, Teresa of Avila, trans. by E. Allison Peers, 2004 Image Books, Doubleday,NY, Chapt. 11

4 Teresa of Avila: Mystical Writings, ed. Tessa Bielecki, 1999, Crossword Publishing Company, NY. p.129

Teresa's Continued Struggles

As the political winds shifted in Spain, Teresa and John of the Cross came under scrutiny by the older order of the Carmelites. Further work on the convents of the Reformed Carmelites was abruptly stopped. In 1577, Teresa was forced into an isolated retirement and chose one of her convents in Toledo.

In Toledo, Teresa could only correspond by letter with her convents to advise them about their problems. There was very little she could do for them. Teresa was weighed down by troubles and anxieties for the nuns and friars of the Reform. The whole work of the Reform was about to fall into ruin.

At this difficult time in her life, she was told by Father Gracian to write another book. He asked her to "reduce the mystic experiences of her reunion with God to a systematic presentation, suitable for the instruction of her nuns."

As an outbreak of influenza went through Spain, Teresa fell ill. When she recovered, many of her old symptoms had returned in full force. She said she suffered from "noises and swollen rivers rushing within her brain, which made it almost impossible to write."[1]

In spite of her miserable conditions, she focused on writing, rising above her situation to produce *The Interior Castle*. No trace of her hardship is found in this masterpiece. It describes states of prayer, bliss, and mystical, spiritual experiences; culminating in her described "union with God."

---

1 Fulop-Miller, Rene, The Saints That Moved the World, Reprint ed. 1991, Ayer Co. Pub., N.H., p.419

Teresa was setting out a private path for each of her followers. Any spiritual seeker could follow her instructions and move up through the different levels of the interior, spiritual castle.

In 1579, Teresa was allowed to leave the convent in Toledo. During the last three years of her life, she returned to her work: visiting her convents, and resuming the founding of new ones. In all, seventeen women's convents and as many men's cloisters were founded by Teresa and John of the Cross.

What We Can Learn From Saint Teresa

It is easy to see our own pain as so much worse than everyone else's. We use it as an excuse to not take the actions that we should and blame our shortcomings on the pain.

When we look at the life of Saint Teresa, we can no longer fool ourselves into such delusion. No matter how bad our lives are, hers was worse. Yet Teresa chose to see the tremendous pain as an asset: her advantage. We can too. We can use our own struggles with pain as a powerful tool just as she did.

The strength Teresa developed from handling her physical pain gave her great mental, emotional and spiritual strength to handle her other problems. Her focus on the big picture instead of her pain made her a powerful leader.

Teresa's life tells us the journey is never over; the struggles and rewards continue for a lifetime. It was not one particular act, but the constant effort over her life that added up to her place as one of the most revered leaders and enlightened spiritual masters of the world. Learning to persevere, to enjoy "the heavens," and to search continuously for self-knowledge, is the key to a complete life. "This path of self knowledge must never be abandoned."[1]

1 Teresa of Avila: Mystical Writings, ed. Tessa Bielecki, 1999, Crossword Publishing Company, NY. p.188

Anthony

*A time is coming when men will go mad, and when
they see someone who is not mad, they will attack
him, saying, "You are mad; you are not like us."*[1]

Saint Anthony

Mental Pain Brought Him Greatness

Mental pain is the core component of mental illness.
You can be mentally ill without physical, spiritual, or even
emotional pain, but without mental pain it would be called
something else. We all fight against the voices in our heads
that are not under our control. To win the battle, we need to
turn to the experts. Saint Anthony knew more about the
battle than perhaps anyone who ever lived.

Saint Anthony fought against mental pain for most of
his 105 years. He fought it alone, with no drugs or therapy to
help. His battle was against the whole gamut: doubt, fear,
self talk, hallucinations, and even the devil himself. In the
process, he developed a strength that could overcome any

---

1 Placher,William Carl, Callings: Twenty Centuries Of Christian Wisdom On Vocation, 2005, Wm. B.
Eerdmans Publishing, Grand Rapids, Michigan, p.80

hardship, and an understanding that would change the world.

"The hero of this drama," writes Rene Fulop-Miller of Anthony, "is a valiant fighter against the Enemy, the eternal opponent of man, and at the end of this superhuman struggle the world sees not a cured patient but a victorious saint."[1] It was his ability to understand and overcome those battles that gave him the clarity and presence of mind to come to the aid of an entire civilization.

Anthony chose to live in an environment that had no other distractions but those in his own mind. He knew that the interior battle was his path to enlightenment, and that it could not be won by looking for ways to avoid it. By facing his own demons instead of running away from the battle, Anthony became one of the greatest saints. His life was an inspiration that has not diminished for almost 1,800 years. Although he spent almost 80 of his years alone, he is credited with saving Christianity from total annihilation.

Early Christianity And The Nile

Two centuries before Anthony was born, Saint Mark, one of the twelve apostles and the writer of the book of Mark in the New Testament, traveled to Egypt to spread the word about Jesus Christ. A great multitude of native Egyptians embraced the teachings along with many Jews who lived in Alexandria, one of the great cities of the time. Christianity flourished in the region, and Saint Mark established the Coptic Orthodox Church in Alexandria around 42 A.D. The

---

1 Fulop-Miller, Rene, The Saints That Moved the World, Reprint ed. 1991, Ayer Co. Pub., N.H., p.28-29

scriptures were translated into the local Coptic language and spread to the rural areas.

Alexandria was the site of one of the first universities in the world. Many scholars visited the School of Alexandria to exchange ideas and to communicate directly with the scholars. The scope of this school was not limited to theological subjects; science, mathematics, and humanities were also taught there.[1]

The Nile delta was a busy trading region on the Mediterranean. Agriculture and the seasons of the river determined the wealth and well-being of the culture. The delta was a land of abundance and beauty. The desert bordered this paradise with harsh rock, sand, and dunes. It was unknown: a land apart. Those who went to the desert were not expected to return safely. It was a place for Bedouin nomads and madmen.

In the era before Anthony was born, some of the early Christians practiced asceticism at home or in huts on the edge of the villages. They would fast for long periods, practice self-denial, and abstain from marriage. They immersed themselves in prayers and meditations.[2]

Anthony was among the first generation of hermits who ventured past the edges of their communities. He went far out into the desert. He inspired so many, that for generations, his prescriptions for the silent life of a hermit were emulated by others. Later, when the first monasteries

---

1 http://en.wikipedia.org/wiki/Coptic_Orthodox_Church

2 Butler, E.C., St. Anthony, The Catholic Encyclopedia, 1907, Robert Appleton Company, N.Y.,Volume I, p.553.

were organized, they took Anthony's example as the cornerstone of monastic life.

Anthony's Childhood

Anthony was born in a small village several miles from Alexandria, into a wealthy agricultural family. Anthony grew up knowing the seasons of the Nile River; planting, irrigating, harvesting, and caring for the animals. His parents distrusted most of the schools of the city. They were not comfortable with the languages and customs of the invading Greeks and Romans. They did not speak Greek or Latin; they spoke Coptic.

His parents chose to keep their son away from the culture of bustling Alexandria. He lived at home with his family and grew up as a devoted member of the Coptic Christian church. Anthony remained illiterate throughout his life. What he learned of religion and scripture was read to him.

Anthony was brought up to manage his family's agricultural business. By the time he was a young man, he was entrusted with managing lands and crops, which were like gold in the culture of the Nile. He was a favorite son of the community, and enjoyed the company of many friends.

His parents died when he was about 20 years old. Anthony dutifully took on the responsibilities that came with inheriting his family's wealth. He managed the business well and increased his landholdings. In every way, it looked like he would become a leader within his community.

One day, scripture read aloud by a priest had an immediate impact on Anthony. It felt like the words were aimed directly at him. "If you want to be perfect, go, sell what you have and give to the poor, and you will have treasures in heaven; and come, follow Me."[1]

Anthony proceeded to follow those instructions to the letter. He sold off his land and property, made arrangements for the care of his sister, distributed all of his wealth to the poor, and began preparing for the life of a hermit.

His community was unable to dissuade him. They expected Anthony to grow up to be a strong leader in their community and were completely surprised that he would turn away from that destiny and live as a hermit.

The priests of the time had land, families and homes, so they could not guide him on his new path. They were no more adept at the life of an ascetic than Anthony. He wandered the outskirts of the city until he found an old ascetic hermit living in a hut. The old man took Anthony in for awhile, and showed him how to survive in the life he had chosen.

The old man taught Anthony the necessity of living a balanced life that included work and prayer. Anthony quickly learned how to weave mats and baskets. This meant he would have something to offer in exchange for food. The old man gave Anthony a thick tunic of camel hair, which would protect from both heat and cold. Anthony learned to make simple meals of bread, water and dried fruit.

---

1 Bible, King James Version, Matthew 19:21

After this period of initiation, Anthony set out to devote his life to God.[1]

Anthony's Life In The Desert

Anthony walked away from the lush, protective life of the river valley and into the harsh, barren desert. He was full of youthful enthusiasm and confidence in himself.

After walking for many hours, the only thing he could see was more sand in every direction. He stumbled upon a large bramble bush that would serve as his shelter for the night.

As Anthony started to fall asleep, he had the first of many visions that would haunt him for the rest of his life. A beautiful young woman came out of nowhere and laid down beside him. She caressed him and made every sort of inviting and enticing gesture to get his attention.

He knew this was an agent of the devil, meant to distract him and keep him from his goal. He spoke out and admonished the devil for trying to tempt him with beauty and sex. The young woman persisted relentlessly through the night. He turned away, again and again, praying to be rescued from this temptation until the vision subsided and then disappeared altogether.[2]

He realized he was not protected enough on the open dunes, so he decided on a very unusual idea. He had seen the distant mountains where there were old tombs carved in

---

1 Fulop-Miller, Rene, The Saints That Moved the World, Reprint ed. 1991, Ayer Co. Pub., N.H., p.28

2 Ibid., p. 26

the rock. He thought the tombs would make an excellent refuge. They would be difficult to reach, so he asked a friend to accompany him on the trip.

The Egyptian culture saw life on earth as transitory, and Egyptian tombs had everything necessary for the life after this one. These chambers, cut out of the rock face of the cliffs, were large and spacious, with high ceilings. They were completely protected from the outside elements of heat, cold and wind. After all, these were tombs, and people did not usually open them or go inside. It was as unusual for Anthony's time as it would be for ours.[1]

Anthony's loyal friend agreed that he would return every month and bring a little bread and water. In exchange, Anthony would trade the mats that the old man taught him to make.

As the door closed behind Anthony, his difficulties began in earnest. Anthony was tempted with thoughts about the life he left behind. He wondered about the welfare of his sister, and missed her. There were foods that he would miss, and many comforts he was accustomed to in his former home. In short, he had doubts and moments of regret.

He was however, determined. Anthony strengthened his will by repeating phrases from scriptures that would help him keep in the present moment. He resolved to live each day as though yesterday did not matter. This practice gave him strength to fight another day.

As Anthony began his routine of meditations and prayer, he noticed that he could not get through the day

---

1 Fulop-Miller, Rene, *The Saints That Moved the World*, Reprint ed. 1991, Ayer Co. Pub., N.H., p.30

without distraction. It seemed as though his adversary was always waiting for his mind to wander. It began as vicious thoughts in his head, distractions of sounds, and bits of wind brushing by his shoulders. As soon as he lost his concentration, it was as though the door had opened to let the devil in.

The visions became increasingly bizarre and frightful. The creatures painted on the walls of the tomb came alive. The phantoms took the form of wild beasts, wolves, lions, snakes, scorpions, and mythical creatures. Every day, Anthony banished all of them from his cave.[1] They returned every time Anthony lost his focus. He was beaten by wings of birds from above, the paws of large lions swiping across his face, and all kinds of other attacks. This went on night and day, making it impossible to rest.

Anthony could not withstand the constant onslaught. He fell down, exhausted, and lapsed into a coma. When his friend arrived at the cave to bring him food and water, he found Anthony near death. He picked him up and brought him back to his village.

Many people in the village came when they heard the news. Anthony was so still and unresponsive that they presumed he was dead. They took him to the church, and many villagers offered to stay with the body overnight.

Anthony woke up while they were all sleeping. He let his good friend know he was going to go back to his tomb. Without waking anyone else, he left and returned to the desert. He may have lost a battle, but he was beginning to

---

1 http://www.copticchurch.org/StAnthonyGreat.htm

understand his tormentor and he felt stronger than ever before.

Anthony laughed when the visions began to return. "If any of you have any authority over me, only one would have been sufficient to fight me."[1] He understood the limits of their power over him.

He learned to live with the voices in his head, and visions of every imaginable kind. Ever shifting and changing, the visions did not cease. Over time, Anthony strengthened his ability to focus; it cut through all of this and kept him ever present in a state of prayer.

Anthony seemed to have won the battle against the devil's cohorts. He spent his days and nights in meditations and prayer. If there were distractions, he had no discomfort or fear from them; he stayed in the present moment.

Finally, the devil himself showed up. If Anthony thought he understood the power of the devil, he had underestimated him. He cried out to the devil that he was safe, within the protection of his faith and the devil could not harm him. The devil determined that Anthony was lost to him and decided to kill him.

The very walls began to tremble. Lions, leopards, bears, and bulls began tearing into the walls. Anthony was filled with horror. Walls were leaning, crumbling, and moving above his head. Snakes and scorpions surrounded his feet. The walls of the tomb were sliding on their foundations. The earth was shaking and roaring. Anthony

---

1 http://www.copticchurch.org/StAnthonyGreat.htm

cringed on his knees as he saw the vaulted ceiling was about to collapse in on him. This was surely his last moment.

But he had been at this for 16 years! He would rather die than give up his beliefs. No adversary could make him do otherwise. In an instant, the devil and his minions suddenly disappeared.

The ceiling opened above him. Anthony experienced bright light surrounding him and the entire tomb became quiet. He asked "Where were you my Lord Jesus? Why did you not come sooner to assist me?" He heard a voice reply "Anthony, I was near you all the time. I was at your side, and I have seen your fight, and because you have withstood your enemy, I will always protect you."[1]

Anthony understood that he had won. He believed that God would never abandon him, and would protect him for the rest of his life. He understood his time there was finished and he emerged from the tomb.

Modern psychiatry would put the whole battle in terms of hallucinations and mental illness. Anthony's battles are identical in many ways to the constant visions of suicide that many of us confront. But, as Goethe said, "Why should we search for the meaning of phenomena, when the phenomena themselves teach us the lesson?"[2] As I said in the *Is My Experience Valid?* chapter, it is not the hardships we face that matter, it is what we become as a result of facing them.

---

1 Fulop-Miller, Rene, The Saints That Moved the World, Reprint ed. 1991, Ayer Co. Pub., N.H., p. 33

2 Fulop-Miller, Rene, The Saints That Moved the World, Reprint ed. 1991, Ayer Co. Pub., N.H., p.29

The Sage On The Mountain

Anthony felt more confident than ever that he had chosen the correct path. He felt liberated by his triumph over the devil. At 36 years old, he was more committed than ever to a life of an ascetic.

Anthony stopped in the village to make arrangements for someone to bring him food and water every six months in exchange for his mats and baskets. He asked that he not be disturbed. It would be sufficient if they would just leave it outside his door. He had chosen a solitary life. He would no longer be visited by his friend on a monthly basis.

Near the top of the mountain were old stone walls of a fortress. Behind the walls were rooms of the old fortress, carved into the rock. This was going to be Anthony's home for the next 20 years.

He was not alone in the fort. First he had to go about housecleaning, getting out all the scorpions, reptiles, bugs, and other creatures that lived there. He had to ignore the numerous goblins, tramps, and troll-like spirits that called the old fort their home too. Their primary goal was to upset Anthony or distract him, or to simply make sure he knew they were there. But compared to his fight with the devil, it was just a minor nuisance.

Within the year, the people of the village began to talk about an odd mystery developing. When they would drop off supplies outside the room where Anthony lived, they heard a loud din of voices, scolding, laughing, and carrying on. They could never tell where all the noise was coming from. The entire room of spirits was causing a ruckus so loud that even the villagers could hear it.

When they peered through cracks in the door, they saw only Anthony. He was sitting still, absorbed in meditation and prayer. They were in awe of the man inside and began to tell others. Soon, there was a small gathering around the entrance at all times.

Anthony came out one day and saw the crowd at his door. He had not been out for more than six months. They expected a weary, insane, famished and fragile hermit to emerge. Instead, they were greeted by an energized, healthy, serene, and enlightened man. He was hailed as a hero and the legend of Anthony began to spread throughout the region.[1]

Soon, Anthony was surrounded by novice ascetic monks, wishing to learn from the master. Anthony realized that he would have to help these devoted souls, if nothing else than to keep them from going crazy from the thoughts which plagued them in isolation:

"What condemns us is not that thoughts enter into us but that we use them badly; indeed, through our thoughts we can be shipwrecked, and through our thoughts we can be crowned."[2]

As Anthony's reputation grew, people came from far and wide to be healed of all kinds of illnesses of the body, mind, and soul. The novices gathered around him, seeking

---

1 Athanasius: Select Works and Letters, Volume IV of Nicene and Post Nicene Fathers, Series II, Philip Schaff and Henry Wace, editors. 1892, Christian Literature Publishing Co., N.Y., p. 200

2 The Wisdom of the Desert Fathers, trans.by Benedicta Ward, 1986, Cisterian Publications, NY, p.29.

advice and help in their spiritual quest. Anthony's kindness and compassion showed in the hours he spent in this new vocation, even though he preferred to hide alone in his cave.[1]

Anthony Brings His Wisdom To Alexandria

The time was coming when the world would need Anthony. In Alexandria, the Christians had fallen under the persecution of the Romans. They were being asked to recant their faith. Those who refused were imprisoned and fed to the lions in the colosseum.

In 312 AD, at sixty-one years old, Anthony came to Alexandria for the first time in his life. As he walked into the streets of Alexandria, it was as foreign and distracting as any vision he had ever had. He saw meats, fruits, spices, and vegetables of every variety, along with costumes and textiles of unbelievable color and texture. There were magicians, artists, musicians, and entertainers at every corner. It was a masterpiece of distraction, yet Anthony was there for only one purpose: to give comfort and confidence to those being persecuted because of their Christian faith.

It is described as a miracle that Anthony walked untouched past the guards, through prisons and labor camps. The tall, erect, youthful-looking man, with his long white beard, white robe and staff, was unearthly in his appearance. No one dared to apprehend him. Even the

---

1 Fulop-Miller, Rene, The Saints That Moved the World, Reprint ed. 1991, Ayer Co. Pub., N.H., p.40

governor of the region would not send out his troops against him.[1]

He did everything that he could to bless his people and give them courage, knowing that many would die in this persecution.

Within a year, the reign of Maximinus Daia was overthrown by Constantine and the persecutions ended. Constantine had already brought religious tolerance for Christians to the Roman Empire in Europe, and his troops brought the same tolerance to Alexandria.

His mission completed, Anthony returned to his home in the mountains. When Constantine visited Alexandria, four years later, he immediately sought out Anthony for his endorsement and his advice.[2]

After his meeting with Constantine, Anthony returned to the desert. He wanted to avoid his former retreat on Mt. Pispir because it had attracted so many pilgrims. Traveling with a group of Bedouins, he went deeper into the desert until he came to an oasis. He found a cave at the edge of the oasis and made it his home. He was so far into the desert that most people could never find him.

Saint Anthony Saves Christianity

Throughout the Christian world, factions had arisen challenging the concept of Jesus as part of the Holy Trinity and the Son of God. This challenge was turning communities

---

1 Fulop-Miller, Rene, The Saints That Moved the World, Reprint ed. 1991, Ayer Co. Pub., N.H., p.45

2 History of Christianity in Egypt/Constantine, interoz.com/egypt/chiste1.htm

and families against each other. There would be no peace until the Church could answer this question once and for all.

In 325 AD, the Council of Nicaea met to decide the fate of Christianity. Bishops came from all over the empire to make the final decision. Constantine was very involved, and of course sided with those who believed in Jesus Christ. Those who followed Arius believed that Jesus was only a man, and therefore could not speak for God.

After vigorous debate, The Council of Nicaea wrote the Nicene Creed:

> "We believe in one God, the Father Almighty, Maker of heaven and earth, and of all things visible and invisible. And in one Lord Jesus Christ, the only-begotten Son of God..."[1]

Not everyone viewed the council or the pope as infallible. Arius continued to attract followers. The Arian belief that Jesus was just a man was growing. Over the next few years, the Nicene Creed was disputed to the point that it was no longer accepted. Christianity once again was faced with annihilation. "If the Arians had won, [Christianity] would have dwindled away into legend."[2]

The debate came to a head in Alexandria. Out of desperation, Athanasius, the primary Bishop of the region and a close friend of Anthony, asked Anthony to come and attest to the divinity of Jesus Christ.

---

1 http://www.newadvent.org/cathen/11049a.htm

2 Fulop-Miller, Rene, The Saints That Moved the World, Reprint ed. 1991, Ayer Co. Pub., N.H., p.61

Once again, the tall, erect saint with the long white beard arrived in the city. This time, people of every faith and ethnic group ran to meet him. They knew the legends of this great man and his powers. They followed him as he made his way through the grand city and waited anxiously to hear what he would say.

What he said would not surprise those who have followed his story, but it rang out over the crowd with so much certainty that the masses knelt in prayer. He said simply "He is God - I have seen him. I have SEEN Him!"[1] Anthony did for the Christians what none of their bishops had been able to do. He gave them confidence in their faith, which is the real power behind the Nicene Creed.

Athanasius begged Anthony to stay and implored him that the church needed him among men. But Anthony felt that his insight and wisdom came from his life of renunciation, and that he would lose his insight if he stayed among people in the city. When he left Alexandria, the Bishop Athanasius gave Anthony his mantle as a show of admiration and devotion. Years later, when Athanasius became the Pope, he would write the biography of Saint Anthony.[2]

Anthony's Life As A Saint

Anthony would go out from his cave only once more. He went in search of the first desert hermit, Paul of Thebes. Paul had spent almost ninety years in the desert, and was

---

1 Fulop-Miller, Rene, The Saints That Moved the World, Reprint ed. 1991, Ayer Co. Pub., N.H., p. 60

2 Butler, E.C., St.Anthony, The Catholic Encyclopedia, 1907, Robert Appleton Company, N.Y, Vol. I p.553

113 years old. There were legends surrounding Paul, but no one had seen him in years.

In the story by Saint Jerome; God asked Anthony to visit, so Paul could spend his last days in the company of a spiritual man, and not just among the animals of the desert.[1]

The desert was different for Anthony ever since he had won his battle with the devil. He was met with only love and assistance. Supernatural creatures that were half human and half animal appeared to show Anthony the way. They kept him on the route toward Paul's cave. These visions were magnificent, friendly, and helpful. Instead of tormenting him, they acted as valuable guides, giving direction and protection.

Anthony was able to arrive in time to see Paul, and spent a day speaking with him before he died. When Paul died, Anthony wrapped him in the mantle that Athanasius had given him, and watched as two lions appeared and dug Paul's grave.[2]

After returning home, Anthony was transformed into a light-filled and radiant example of love. Nearing 100 years old, Anthony was the ever-young, limber, tall man he had always been. He was now gently compassionate, turning his monks toward the way of love; no longer stressing the ascetic way of life.

One day, when Anthony was filling water jugs at the spring, he had a vision. As he turned from the spring, the

---

1 Fulop-Miller, Rene, The Saints That Moved the World, Reprint ed. 1991, Ayer Co. Pub., N.H., p.63

2 The Life of Paulus the First Hermit by St. Jerome, www.newadvent.org/fathers/3008.htm

way back to his cave became a field of green, with knee high ripening wheat. He felt the grains in his hands, and remembered his life as a young farmer. He realized that the spring could support fields of wheat in the valley. It was a vision of what he could create, so he began the next day.

After borrowing some tools, Anthony created an entire irrigation system and planted his seeds. Within weeks, he was looking at wheat sprouting in the fields. In a few months, he had his first crop. He made his own bread; enough for all who came to visit him.[1]

At 105 years old, Anthony knew his time on earth was over. He told his closest disciples to spread the word, so that his many followers would have a last opportunity to visit. From all regions of Egypt, and all walks of life, they came to see Anthony. So many arrived, that they made a large encampment around the area. Many were ascetics and hermits who had followed his example.

Anthony walked lovingly among them, giving last bits of advice, and reminding them to walk in the way of love. His bread was divided until it had fed all of them.

Saint Anthony is often called the Father of the Western Monastic orders.

Learning From Our Mental Conditions

When "normal" people read about Saint Anthony's visions, they often wonder what it must have been like, or if the visions were "real." Those of us who share Anthony's gift know exactly what it was like. My visions,

---

1 Fulop-Miller, Rene, The Saints That Moved the World, Reprint ed. 1991, Ayer Co. Pub., N.H., p.68

hallucinations, voices, and delusions are completely "real" in the context of how they affect my life.

Anthony's life has one defining characteristic. He faced every aspect of his mind, learned from it, and came to understand the "real" world better than anyone. Nearly a century in the desert did not render Anthony completely insane and dysfunctional. To the contrary, Anthony was viewed as wise, disciplined, and a master of his thoughts and actions. Each time he came to Alexandria, he brought clarity to confusion. He walked untouched by the confusion and turmoil of city life, because he had seen much worse in his own head.

If you face your mental conditions and learn to understand them, they will lose their power. In the movie "A Beautiful Mind," Dr. John Nash reminds his colleagues that the companion visions are always there - "I just choose to ignore them."[1]

I believe ignoring them is the wrong approach. John Nash accepted a diminished life that had his best days behind him. Anthony became better until his last breath. The difference: Anthony chose to learn from his experiences instead of avoiding or denying them.

With understanding, the same capacity of the mind to create visions can be turned to an advantage. Instead of completely avoiding, denying, or masking the symptoms, it is important also to face them from time to time, and to learn from them.

---

1 "A Beautiful Mind," 2001, Universal Pictures

On some level, each individual must know what his or her own weaknesses are, and do what is necessary to overcome them. Fear decreases with knowledge. Control increases with understanding. Good visions can give us hope, encouragement and a desire to live; even painful visions can fortify us simply through the experience of surviving them. Each individual needs knowledge of his or her own strength and capacity for this. Facing our mental conditions will give us knowledge of our true strengths and our full potential.

Milarepa

Do you not fear the miseries
You experienced in the past?
Surely you will feel much pain
If misfortunes attack you?
The woes of life succeed one another
Like the sea's incessant waves -
One has barely passed, before
The next one takes its place.
Until you are liberated, pain
and pleasure come and go at random
Like passers-by encountered in the street.[1]

Milarepa

Emotional Pain Creates One Of Tibet's Great Sages

Most people associate depression with only emotional pain. When you tell someone you are depressed, they don't think of physical, mental, or spiritual pain. Emotional pain is what most people think depression is. Even though this view is pervasive, it isn't correct. Nevertheless, emotional

---

1 http://www.kagyu-asia.com/l_mila_t_karma_samsara.html

pain is a component of depression and the experiences of sadness, regret, remorse, and guilt can pull us into deep despair.

Sometimes our success in struggling with depression relies on our ability to put the past behind us. There is a time when it is necessary to stop carrying burdens of remorse and guilt into the future. Many times, we cannot remake or redo things that went horribly wrong. Whatever the circumstances, we have to come to terms with them and accept ourselves and the situation we face today.

Milarepa is a widely revered and loved Buddhist sage from Tibet. His story is inspiring because through acceptance, devotion, perseverance, and commitment, he survived his trials of deep emotional depression. He was able to overcome the actions of his past by drastically changing his life.

Tibet In The Eleventh Century

The English word Tibet is derived from the Persian word meaning "the heights." Tibet is the high and mountainous region bordering India, Nepal, Bhutan, Myanmar, Russia, and China. Most of the Himalaya mountain range lies within Tibet.

The lamas of the Tibetan region have taught various forms of Buddhism that they incorporated from India. They established numerous monasteries to pass on specific lineages of teaching. They have been spiritual advisors to the Mongol kings of Tibet and China since Buddhism was first brought into Tibet.

Milarepa's Childhood

Milarepa was born into a good family with wealth in agricultural land and animals. His father had acquired wealth through trade, and the home that Milarepa was born into was considered the cornerstone of the region. Everyone came to his father for help with money or supplies, and were generously taken care of.

When Milarepa was only around 7 years old, his father died. Before he died, the father instructed the uncle and aunt to care for his family and his properties until Milarepa reached the age of maturity at 15. At that time, Milarepa was to inherit all of his father's wealth and land.

Milarepa's uncle quickly manipulated the situation and reduced Milarepa, his mother, and his sister to household servants of the lowest rank, usurping all of their wealth. Milarepa suddenly became a servant in his own home.

He was betrayed again when his uncle refused to turn over the lands to Milarepa when he turned 15. The uncle treated his mother and sister very badly, and suggested he had used up all of their wealth caring for them since the father had died. He threw the family off the estate, and forced them to live on the charity of other relatives.[1]

Milarepa was able to forget his miserable circumstances from time to time. He was singing in the fields one day, when his mother heard him, and chastised him for being happy when she was so miserable. She questioned if

---

1 The Life of Milarepa, trans. by Lobsang P. Lhalungpa, 1992, Penguin, N.Y., p.20

he understood the hardship that she and his sister Peta were going through.

His mother was filled with rage and the desire for revenge. She insisted that Milarepa go out and learn the black arts from a good teacher and seek revenge for their misfortune. Milarepa's mother threatened she would kill herself if he didn't do this.

It was through this desperate request by his mother, that Milarepa first chose sorcery, revenge and retribution. He studied with a well-known sorcerer, becoming skilled in the rituals for invoking lightning and hailstorms.[1] When he was well prepared to take revenge, he returned and rained down hailstorms and lightning for days. The devastation was unimaginable. He succeeded in completely destroying all of his relatives.

His mother ran about with a banner claiming victory over those who had treated her so harshly. She was gloating with cruelty and joy at the revenge her son had brought. The remaining villagers thought about killing her, but instead decided on sending out a search party to find Milarepa and kill him. Milarepa had exacted his mother's revenge, but in that act he lost all hope of ever going home again.

Milarepa decided to return to his studies with an altogether different perspective. He longed for spiritual knowledge and practice. He worried greatly over the bad karma he had incurred through his evil actions and could think of nothing else. Milarepa moved from teacher to teacher in his quest for spiritual fulfillment.

---

1 The Life of Milarepa, trans. by Lobsang P. Lhalungpa, 1992, Penguin, N.Y., p.26

Years Of Study With Marpa The Translator

Marpa was the greatest Buddhist teacher in Tibet at the time. He enthusiastically sought Buddhist instruction in India, where he was accepted with the great Indian mystic teacher Naropa and learned the "Six yogas of Naropa" along with Naropa's encyclopedic knowledge and wisdom of the Buddhist traditions.[1] Naropa formally declared Marpa to be his successor, although he had other major disciples in India.

Upon his return to Tibet, Marpa spent many years translating Buddhist scriptures and made a major contribution to the transmission of the complete *buddhadharma* (Buddhist teaching) into the Tibetan language. Marpa is also credited with the translation of Vajrayana and Mahamudra techniques of realization.

Marpa was very happy about the possibility of instructing Milarepa: he had been given a premonition in dreams that Milarepa was the disciple who would inherit his lineage.[2] Marpa knew from his dreams that Milarepa had a good heart and great mental and spiritual powers. He also knew that the accumulated bad karma must be dealt with. He understood that this particular disciple had extremely powerful gifts that had been put to the wrong use. Marpa was obligated to put Milarepa through arduous training that would work off his bad karma. Even more importantly, Marpa had to be sure that Milarepa would never resort to

---

1 The Life of Milarepa, trans. by Lobsang P. Lhalungpa, 1992, Penguin, N.Y., p.214

2 The Life of Milarepa, trans. by Lobsang P. Lhalungpa, 1992, Penguin, N.Y., p.43

that negative use of his powers again, no matter how desperate his circumstances became.

Marpa decided to have his student build a stone tower and then, just as he was nearing completion, Marpa would tell him to tear it down and put all the stones back where they came from. Over and over again, each time seemingly very sincere, Marpa made this request for Milarepa to build one tower and then another, for some specific purpose. When it was nearing completion, Marpa would point out its flaws and tell Milarepa to tear it down. The work was excruciatingly difficult and wore Milarepa's body and mind to complete exhaustion each time. Although this seems like the archetypal story of the master removing all pride and ego from the novice, in Milarepa's case it represents something more.

Marpa never explained to Milarepa that he was forced to repeatedly push Milarepa into emotional depression to clear his karmic troubles. He never explained anything. Every time that Milarepa showed up for instruction in spiritual teachings with other students, Marpa turned him away cruelly, telling him he was not worthy and calling him "Great Magician" while beating him in front of other students. Milarepa never understood why he was being rejected and mistreated. He only wanted to learn the path to enlightenment, but he was not even allowed to study. He saw many students go ahead of him. He was humiliated, discouraged, and heartbroken.

Milarepa thought, "Was this punishment for the murders I had committed through sorcery and for the destruction of numerous crops by my hailstorms? Did [Marpa] know that I would never be able to practice the

Dharma? Or was it through lack of compassion that he would not teach me? Whatever it may be, of what use is this human body which, without religion, only accumulates defilement? Should I kill myself?"[1]

Milarepa was left in a state of grief and confusion every time this happened. He was often reduced to tears that only brought more chastisement. Marpa would remind Milarepa of the great feats and mortifications other famous Lamas underwent during their spiritual training. This was Marpa's way of letting Milarepa know that there was no tolerance for self pity, and Milarepa had only himself to blame for his lack of progress.

After yet another rebuke from Marpa, Milarepa recounts that "I was not hurt, but was filled with grief and longed to die."[2] Milarepa was so discouraged, he decided that Marpa would never be willing to teach him. He had been dutiful, respectful, and very devoted to Marpa, even though he did not understand what was happening most of the time. Sadly, his will was giving out and he felt he should just go away and try to find another teacher.

Milarepa never discussed his leaving with Marpa. Without telling him, Milarepa accepted letters of recommendation and a gift from Marpa's wife as a way to get into the school of one of Marpa's disciples. He left without saying a word to Marpa, and went in search of his new teacher.

---

1 The Life of Milarepa, trans. by Lobsang P. Lhalungpa, 1992, Penguin, N.Y., p.54

2 Ibid.

He was warmly accepted by Lama Ngogpa because of the letters and gifts from Marpa. Lama Ngogpa believed that Milarepa had Marpa's blessing, and was very honored to take on one of Marpa's students.

Lama Ngogpa began the lessons and taught Milarepa some meditation techniques; setting him in a cave with food and water, and giving him time to practice. Although he followed the instructions dutifully, he made no progress. Even the teacher did not understand why this student was not progressing after being given these simple meditation techniques.

Milarepa began to suspect on his own that his lack of progress was because he had not told his teacher the full story about how he left Marpa. He did not mention it to his teacher, but continued his efforts. Not accepting his past and lying about it by "leaving it out" was making it impossible to progress.

By the time the teacher was beginning to figure it out, they were summoned before Marpa at the time of a big festival.[1]

On their arrival at Marpa's house, Marpa berated Milarepa, and chastised the Lama Ngogpa for accepting Milarepa as a student. He yelled and screamed and beat Milarepa in front of everyone gathered. This final humiliation was so great that Milarepa ran to another part of the compound to kill himself. Lama Ngogpa understood the depth of his suffering and despair so he stayed with Milarepa, refusing to leave his side.

---

1 http://www.cosmicharmony.com/Av/Milarepa/Milarepa.htm

Marpa saw that he could not insist on any further emotional harm to Milarepa. He called Lama Ngogpa and Milarepa back to the house and made a detailed recounting of all that had occurred from the time he first met his worthy disciple. He had been forced to use controlled anger, he explained, with an aim to contribute to the spiritual development of Milarepa.[1] He explained the necessity of plunging Milarepa into this deep emotional depression eight times, to remove all of his bad karma. Marpa now accepted Milarepa as a true student and began to teach him the way of enlightenment.

The Path To Realization

Milarepa progressed very quickly in his meditations, because he had built up so much discipline, fortitude, will power and perseverance over the years. He became a very close and favorite disciple and was told he would reach enlightenment in this lifetime. Milarepa enjoyed the happiness of being with Marpa, who now treated him as a favorite son. He lived in contentment, satisfied with the spiritual insights that were coming to him and the comfort of being loved and well cared for.

A few years later, Milarepa had a series of lifelike dreams that dragged him back into his sorrowful past again. He saw his mother's house and fields burning, her bones in the middle of the ashes, and his sister wandering aimlessly in the village, homeless, and deranged. These images pervaded his consciousness and made it impossible to meditate. This went on for a week before he woke up early

---

1 http://tibetanfoundation.org/biographies/milarepa.php

one morning, rushed in, and finding Marpa asleep, woke him to beg for his wisdom and ask permission to leave for his village.

Milarepa went to his village in search of his family. When he arrived, he found that he was not in time to save his mother. Everything was exactly as the dream had showed him. His entire body and soul grieved in deep sorrow and remorse for all the trouble he had caused, and the loss of his family.

However, when he began meditating, he felt a wave of peace come over him. He realized that through the depths of his deepest emotional depressions, he had gained the ability to change himself. He understood that he could now put his burdens down. Filled with an overwhelming peace, he felt liberated from his past.

Milarepa's realization previewed his coming enlightenment and complete liberation. He was free to attain his goal. Exchanging his house and land for some food, he left his former homeland forever, and proceeded to the first of many caves he was to inhabit over the remainder of his life. He consecrated over 20 caves in the Himalayas with his peaceful meditations.

Milarepa radiated a spiritual light like a beacon, drawing vast numbers of followers toward the light, and dispelling the darkness of selfishness and ignorance.[1] Many students were attracted to him and he took on many disciples. He taught the teachings handed down from Naropa and Marpa. Through the teachings, he was credited

---

1 The Life of Milarepa, trans. by Lobsang P. Lhalungpa, 1992, Penguin, N.Y., p.58

with the liberation and enlightenment of many people. He is revered for his emphasis on completing good works and right behavior.

What Milarepa Can Mean To Us

Milarepa's feelings became a powerful agent for personal growth. If he had not experienced such remorse and guilt, he would not have desired to change.

Marpa was an astute and insightful teacher: he knew emotional pain could be used to an advantage, to transform Milarepa from someone capable of death and destruction into a saint. Marpa understood that he could use Milarepa's suffering as a way to develop deep compassion in his protege, so he would always see his responsibility for how his actions affected others.

Milarepa's story is also inspiring because he persevered even in the face of the trials which Marpa presented to him. Milarepa could have walked away from these trials at any time and reverted to his old ways.

His insight allowed him to choose peace over all of his burdens of the past. He had to be willing to accept that he could not undo the past, nor could he carry this grief with him forever. He could not walk into his future of complete liberation without letting go. It was the overwhelming peace that he felt while meditating in the ashes of his home, that taught him this final lesson.

Emotional depression can be an agent of change in our own lives. Instead of asking, "Why is this happening to me and how can I stop it?" we need to be asking, "What can I learn from this?" The old paradigm is for us to avoid emotional pain at all costs while remaining ignorant of the lessons that are available to us. If we replace ignorance and fear with the deep understanding that comes from introspection and changing the way we look at our experiences, we too can use our emotional depression as an agent of change.

John of the Cross

"By this road, because it is so narrow, dark and terrible, they are far fewer that journey, but its benefits are far greater without comparison."[1]

Saint John of the Cross

Spiritual Pain:
The Dark Night Of The Soul

The questions that come with deep despair are not easy ones. "What's the point? Why me? If there is a god, where is he?" Deep, spiritual despair is a component of depression that is often not discussed. It often is the worst and most misunderstood part. If more people understood this kind of despair, maybe there would be someone to talk to about it. For the most part, we are left without a guide on this part of the journey.

The Dark Night of the Soul, by Saint John of the Cross, has almost become synonymous with depression because it describes feelings to which we can relate. The wisdom of this book has been reinterpreted through the ages by many

---

1 The Dark Night of the Soul, translated by E. Allison Peers, 1990 Random House, New York, pp. 49 – 50

authors of books of a spiritual nature. In the field of
psychiatry, authors have used the title or mentioned it in
their own books and articles. Written by Saint John of the
Cross in the 16th century, *The Dark Night of the Soul* defines
the stages of spiritual despair. In clear and even progression,
it lays out the journey through the deepest of dark nights
and guides us back. This is the story of the man that took
this journey and offered to be our guide.

John of the Cross was after enlightenment his entire
life. He witnessed it in Saint Teresa of Avila, so he knew it
was possible for him also. Like Saint Teresa, his goal was
"union with God." As a scholar, he seems to have always
known by intuition that he would not find it in books.

John's lifelong desire to seek out quiet spots of
contemplation never left him. It wasn't until his dark night
that he realized that even if he found the perfect place for
contemplation, his meditations and prayers wouldn't give
him enlightenment. What he didn't anticipate was the power
of his spiritual suffering. Nothing in his life was more
painful or more transforming.

Thomas Merton, a Catholic mystic who lived in our
times, reassures us about getting involved with John of the
Cross. "John of the Cross, who seems at first sight to be a
saint for the most pure of the Christian elite, may very well
prove to be the last hope of harlots and publicans... His
teaching is not merely a matter of 'Carmelite spirituality,' as
some seem to think. In fact, I would venture to say that he is
the Father of all those whose prayer is an undefined isolation
outside the boundary of 'spirituality.' He deals chiefly with
those who, in one way or another, have been brought face to

face with God in a way that methods cannot account for and books do not explain."[1]

The Dark Night of the Soul was written by someone who had been there. John of the Cross found enlightenment in his own spiritual pain.

Sixteenth Century Spain

John of the Cross would face the same political forces, and same difficulties dealing with them as was described for Teresa of Avila. The 16th century had even more difficulties for the lower classes. For people living in poverty like John, there was a world of suffering. Everyone living in poverty was subject to multiple rounds of famine, plague, and other highly contagious diseases during his or her lifetime. Perhaps the difficult circumstances of his childhood poverty actually assisted John. When he met his fate later in life, he had already experienced incredible loneliness, hunger, and poverty.

Early Childhood

John of the Cross was born in 1542, in a small town not far from Avila. His father died when John was somewhere between two and four years old. His mother was a weaver. She attempted to keep her small family together by moving from village to village, wherever she thought she could make a living. She went to one of the largest trade and mercantile centers of the time, Medina del Campo, but try as she might, she could not keep her family supplied with

---

1 Merton, Thomas, Essay on St. John of the Cross; Saints for Now, ed. by Clare Booth Luce, 1952, Sheed & Ward, London

adequate clothing, housing and food. John's brother Luis died from the hardship and malnutrition, so his mother was forced to put John into an orphanage-school. By this difficult sacrifice on her part, she was able to save him.[1]

The orphanage gave John an education, food and clothes. He was bright, a quick learner, helpful and willing. He was offered jobs working at the church, and later offered a chance to learn skills in the trades. It was expected that this young orphan would take an apprenticeship in carpentry, sculpture, painting or tailoring. John never became proficient enough in one of the trades to complete an apprenticeship. His interests and talents were elsewhere.

He was offered a job at the hospital when he was still a young boy, and worked there for several years. At the hospital, he saw people die from the plague and other diseases. John's compassion, patience, and gentleness, caught the attention of the hospital administrator. This was part of John's character that stayed with him for a lifetime.

Early Aspirations

Don Alonso, the hospital administrator, also noticed John had a passion for reading and was already quite skilled in Latin. He made it possible for John to go on to higher education. This was the beginning of a life devoted to literature and philosophy. He began his studies in humanities at the recently established Jesuit school of Saint Ignatius of Loyola when he was 17.[2]

---

1 http://www.carmelite.com/saints/john/b3.shtml

2 Ibid.

When John graduated from his studies with the Jesuits, he had several opportunities. He was offered ordination and a position working with Don Alonso, and he could have continued with the Jesuits in scholarly pursuits. The socially interactive life of a hospital priest or a scholar didn't appeal to John. Instead, he wanted a quiet life of contemplation. He chose to become a monk at the order of the Carmelites in Medina. As a novice, he would still study, but it would be a life of quiet devotion and prayer.

John always showed a strong desire for a contemplative life of meditation and prayer. However, his unique gifts as a scholar and a leader would mean that he was most often requested to fulfill those roles within the order. He found a way to satisfy both aspects, although not always in a way he would have imagined. John would lead a very complete and rewarding vocational and spiritual life, but he would continue long after he was successful to seek his ultimate spiritual goal of "oneness with God."

University Of Salamanca

The Carmelites realized John's gifts for scholarship and his great intellect. They sent him to the University of Salamanca to return to his studies of theology and philosophy. John arrived in 1564 at this beautiful and busy university center near the Portugal border in western Spain. Many well known professors and students from all around Spain were assembled there. The vibrant society of the university was completely seductive and promising to John at that time.

At the university, John was able to study with Father Luis Ponce de Leon. This turned out to be one of the greatest academic and scholarly influences of his life. Ponce de Leon was only a few years into his position as a professor, but he was very revered and respected. He was a prolific writer, translating classical texts and the Biblical "Song of Solomon." This poem became a favorite for John of the Cross.[1]

John was thoroughly involved in his studies and was appreciated as a scholar. He was engaged on a daily basis in teaching classes, and interacting with students and other scholars.[2] However, he began to be dissatisfied and feel that the constant dissertations and scholastic arguments were leading nowhere. As his university education was concluding, John had to consider his vocational options.

To this young man so caught up in the world of literature, the roles awaiting him as director and administrator in the priesthood were looking less appealing. He was already longing for something more. His goal in life was direct contact with God, one he believed could be reached through isolated contemplation.

Work With Teresa Of Avila

To satisfy his desire for the contemplative life, John returned to the Carmelites, was ordained into the priesthood, and went to celebrate his first Mass in Medina del Campo. He had not yet met the dynamic and persuasive Teresa of Avila who would recruit him for the Reformed Carmelites and convince him to take a leadership role.

---

1 Luis Ponce de Leon, Encyclopedia Britannica, 1911, V16, Page 443

2 http://www.carmelite.com/saints/john/b3a.shtml

Teresa of Avila came to John with a proposition that he become the spiritual director in charge of founding men's monasteries of the Reformed Carmelites, based on the reforms that she had set at the convents for her nuns. She expected that the men's monasteries would be less reclusive, do more teaching, and be more involved with the community in education and spiritual life. She had great confidence that she had found her ally in John.

John was convinced that she offered him what he was looking for. She took seriously his desire for direct spiritual experience, a life of contemplation, and prayer. She shared his desires and told him that she had also been interested in a more introspective life. She shared with him her interest in the Franciscans who were practicing "recollection." She had been greatly inspired by them and was following their practice of interior prayer.[1]

John recognized Teresa for the spiritual dynamo that she was, and knew he would learn a great deal from her. Teresa recognized his learning and scholarship as a marvelous compliment to the devotional life of the order. Teresa's nuns would soon be calling John "God's archives."[2]

In 1568, he took the name of John of the Cross when he joined the Reformed Carmelites, and began building the first monastery. The monastery in Alcala de Henares was specifically located next to the university for the education of the novice monks. John was to guide young novices in their studies and give them spiritual direction. Throughout his

---

1 http://www.carmelite.com/saints/john/b3b.shtml

2 http://www.carmelite.com/saints/john/b3b.shtml

vocation, this would remain his primary assignment - to educate and direct the spiritual life of other monks and nuns.

John was known for his versatility. He would design the architecture to build aqueducts or libraries, work in the quarry, or sweep floors. Although he was highly valued for his scholarship and his spiritual insight, he always set the example that any task was worthy of his attention.

He also made time for all those that were sick and those in poverty. If they were in the community or in the monastery, it was John who first noticed the needs of others and did something about it. He always made room for poor children in the community, and brought them in to educate them. His compassion and kindness were well known. Those novices who came into the convent or monastery from a life of poverty could never afford a new habit or new shoes. John always noticed and went out and bought the items for them. He would attend to the sick and search out special medicines for them.[1]

The ancient Carmelite Rule dictated a life of austerity. John of the Cross set the example and seemed to thrive under it. Teresa of Avila cautioned and pleaded with him to emphasize a balanced life. She needed young university students in her order of priests, and didn't want them to turn away because of harsh living conditions at the monastery. John understood that while he may have associated austerity with purity, he would need to use the attraction of joy and love.

---

1 http://www.carmelite.com/saints/john/b3f.shtml

When Teresa invited John to work directly with her at the Convent of the Incarnation in Avila in 1572, the manner in which their different strengths complimented each other was evident to everyone. John of the Cross saw Teresa elevated to great spiritual heights, and witnessed her "union with God," but she credits him with guiding her during those years.

If he had not witnessed Teresa's union, John of the Cross may not have realized that he really could achieve his goal of oneness with God. He felt he had lived a life of many challenges in poverty, but in the life of the spirit he felt confident in his scholastic achievements, his daily practice, and the luxury of being surrounded by those of a similar consciousness. He was looked up to by those who worked with him, and enjoyed guiding many people through spiritual crisis. John had every opportunity available to him during those years, yet his ultimate challenge of "union with God" was yet to come.

The Dark Night Of The Soul

In December of 1577, John of the Cross was abducted without notice, charges, a trial, or any explanation. He was taken away in the middle of the night to prison. The older Carmelite order was willing to go this far to stop the reform movement and maintain their status quo.[1]

After two weeks, he was not released, but moved to a horrible solitary confinement with no end in sight. He was deprived of light, food, sleep, was unable to bathe, completely exposed to the cold in winter and the heat in

---

1 The Collected Works Of St. John Of The Cross, rvsd. ed.,trans. by Kieran Kavanaugh, 1991, ICS Publications.

summer, and was unable to speak with anyone who knew him. The cell that he was locked up in was so small that he could barely move around. The deprivation of sleep and daylight alone would have made someone with less mental strength go crazy. Someone who had not already known poverty and hunger might have fallen immediately ill and lost the will to live.

John suffered miserably and horribly for months on end. His only interaction with any human being was to be beaten and asked to recant his support of the Reformed Carmelite movement he helped to establish. He simply remained silent.[1]

John of the Cross was able to withstand the physical, emotional, and mental circumstances of his prison. What he could not endure was spiritual deprivation. For him, that was his weak link, and he would have to struggle with it to the very depths of his being.

For those who maintain a spiritual practice and feel they are frequently enjoying the peace of their connection with the divine, to be suddenly without that reassurance is devastating. For John of the Cross to have been deprived of his entire spiritual community - the mass, literature, meditations and prayer - was a greater shock than any other hardship. Had he felt the presence of his God, this total abandonment of spiritual life would have been bearable. However, his prayer and meditations were empty, his soul was denied all pleasure and peace. He was alone and without God.

---

1 Merton, Thomas, Essay on St. John of the Cross; Saints for Now, ed. by Clare Booth Luce, 1952, Sheed & Ward, London

"As silver is tried by fire, and gold in the furnace, so the Lord tries hearts."[1]

The dark, small cell that John of the Cross lived in for nine months was literally and symbolically a deprivation of the senses, the mind, and the heart. Like the state-specific memory of depression, he did not believe it would ever end. This was the proverbial desert.

This is how John of the Cross describes it when the imagination, the will, the intellect, and sense of peace and pleasure are denied the spiritual seeker: "When they believe the sun of Divine favor is shining most brightly, all their interior light is turned to darkness, and the door shut against the source of the sweet spiritual water which they were tasting whenever they desired."[2]

There was no progress in meditation, no feeling in prayer, no connection. For the first time, where there was always comfort, peace, pleasure, and confidence, there was doubt. John would have to question himself: What's the point? Is there a god? No debate or argument in your head can resolve these questions.

"A soul finds no pleasure or consolation in anything."[3] As all else drops away from the senses of the body and the senses of the soul, there is only emptiness.

What can possibly follow this state of complete deprivation? More and more of the same. It may go on for

---

1 Bible, King James Version,1 Prov. 17:3

2 The Dark Night of the Soul, trans. by E. Allison Peers, 1990 Random House, N.Y., Chapt.5-3

3 The Dark Night of the Soul, trans. by E. Allison Peers, 1990 Random House, N.Y., Chapt.9-2

weeks, for months, for years. It is described as a purifying process by John of the Cross. He used the imagery of "night" to describe the agony of depression, desolation, and the feeling of divine abandonment.[1]

Thomas Merton tells us that this is a path without formula, without prescription. "No one becomes a saint without solving the problem of suffering... The saint solves the problem not by a merely speculative solution, not by analyzing, but by suffering. It is a living solution burned in the flesh and in the spirit by fire."[2]

Eventually, this kind of despair becomes a huge, hollowed-out emptiness. From this point forward, the soul will have to find its own way. There is no path to follow. For John of the Cross, this turns into the moment where healing begins. After enduring all that he had for months, he writes that in this space a "yearning for God becomes so great in the soul that the very bones seem to be dried up by their thirst."[3]

Out of this great thirst, John of the Cross describes a rekindling of a love. This love is so pure, subtle, and refined in nature that the soul could not perceive it while it was distracted by the lower consciousness. He describes a healing and awakening from an almost dead state (of the

1 Haase, Albert, O.F.M., Contemplatives and Mystics, Walking with the Saints Magazine, June 2007, AmericanCatholic.org

2 Merton, Thomas, Essay on St. John of the Cross; Saints for Now, ed. by Clare Booth Luce, 1952, Sheed & Ward, London

3 The Dark Night of the Soul, trans. by E. Allison Peers, 1990 Random House, N.Y., Chapt.10-6

lower consciousness) into the higher self. "Thy light will shine in the darkness."[1]

This was the enlightenment of Saint John of the Cross. This was his "union with God" that he had longed for. What his vocation, scholarship, devoted life of prayer, and meditation did not bring him, his dark night brought so profoundly.

He found his "union with God" by facing the challenge of losing all of his beliefs. He had to face his deepest despair and endure it. His writing reminds us that it was not by spiritual pleasures and imaginative meditations, but only by way of this dark night that he arrived. "They are very few that endure and persevere in entering by this straight gate and by the narrow way which leads to life."[2]

During the last few months of his imprisonment, John of the Cross had made such an impression on one of his jailers, that the man had started to bring him paper and pens for writing. In this way, John was able to begin to write the multitude of verses that were in his head. His mind was so flooded with ideas and poetry that it would take him years after he left prison to get it all written.

John of the Cross escaped his solitary confinement and imprisonment nine months after it began. With patience and ingenuity, he was able to determine an escape route. By this time, John of the Cross was in such a weakened state that he probably would have died if he hadn't escaped and received help. A nearby convent was able to help him get to

---

1 The Dark Night of the Soul, trans. by E. Allison Peers, 1990 Random House, N.Y., Chapt.12-4

2 The Dark Night of the Soul, trans. by E. Allison Peers, 1990 Random House, N.Y., Chapt.11-4

where Saint Teresa of Avila was in Toledo. The nuns were able to hide him and keep him hospitalized there until his recovery.

He took out of prison the poetry that he had been able to write down, and the poetry and books that were in his head. After leaving prison and regaining his health, he wrote the *Spiritual Canticle, The Ascent on Mt. Carmel* and *The Dark Night of the Soul*. He wrote many letters and poems; some of them survived in the libraries of the convents and monasteries.[1]

Later Years

The beauty that he brought into literature through his experiences was not the expression of someone who had turned bitter from the struggles and sufferings in life. To the contrary, the poetry of the Spiritual Canticle is full of color, love and life. His lyrical poetry is some of the best in the Spanish language.[2] His descriptions of the path of the spirit toward enlightenment are clear and true.

From the moment of his "union with God," John felt liberated. After escaping prison, he regained his health quickly, and lost no time taking on as many projects as he could. "The soul has to sing of the happy chance of its passage from this dreadful night."[3]

---

1 Zimmerman, Benedict, St. John of the Cross, Catholic Encyclopedia, 1909, Robert Appleton Company, N.Y, Vol.8, p.480, www.NewAdvent.org

2 Thomas Merton, Essay on St. John of the Cross; Saints for Now, ed. by Clare Booth Luce, 1952, Sheed & Ward, London

3 The Dark Night of the Soul, trans. by E. Allison Peers, 1990 Random House, N.Y., Chapt.14-3

As he traveled to his different monasteries, John of the Cross was known for choosing the worst room in the monastery for his own. After his dark night, there was very little that bothered him. He really did not care. Because his spirit had met the ultimate challenge, everything seemed easy for him now.

By contrast, he was very aware of the sufferings of others. He cared personally for men who fell ill while under his direction at the monastery, and would even cook for them. He never asked for special recognition because of his position. Instead it was the opposite. He wanted to be unknown.[1]

In his last "home," a monastery in Ubeda, John was not very well cared for. Father Crisostomo was the administrative director of the monastery and well known in the community. He seemed mostly concerned about his own reputation and status. The sick, holy monk was a nuisance to him, and he let John of the Cross know that he was a burden and an expense to the monastery.

John of the Cross took it on himself to transform this situation as he had done many times before. In his letter to the nuns he wrote: "Do not let what is happening to me, daughters, cause you any grief, for it does not cause me any... Where there is no love, put love, and you will draw out love."[2]

When he knew his death was near, John of the Cross called Crisostomo to him and apologized for being a burden

1 http://www.carmelite.com/saints/john/b3e.shtml

2 Ibid.

on the monastery. Crisostomo was so overwhelmed that he broke into tears and begged forgiveness from John of the Cross. Father Crisostomo's life was changed forever. In his last great suffering, John of the Cross was so compassionate with those around him that their lives were transformed by his love and kindness.

Lessons We Can Learn From Saint John Of The Cross

I have struggled the most with the end of this chapter. There is a tremendous desire to write something meaningful and profound, but I must admit that I cannot come up with anything. Everything I want to write ends up wrong and I don't think there is any integrity in claiming to know something that I don't.

There is a big difference between BEEN there and AM there. With the other saint chapters I can write with authority because I have been there and came to conclusions that have meaning for me. With the Dark Night of the Soul, I AM there and can only hope to find my way out. Like John of the Cross, it has shaken me to the core of my beliefs. Unlike him, mine is not so much a dark night as a seven year twilight of a dull aching pain that seems to go on and on with no end in sight. While I AM there, any conclusion has no meaning or else I would be saying I've BEEN there.

My mind keeps thinking John was lucky that it only lasted nine months. Like getting a tooth pulled, it seems easier to just put up with the short term pain than to drag it out with shots and all. If one intense night would bring it to a conclusion, then bring it on. This slow pain seems so much more to endure when I am too worn out to keep up the fight. But I keep on fighting because there is no other option that makes any sense.

I have wanted to write that my lesson from John was that you don't need to meditate or any other practice, but I intuitively know that to be a lie. It was my years of meditation and deep spiritual practice that gave me the insight and strength to make it this far. I assume it was the accumulation of life experiences that got John through too. I am afraid to admit that I will not make it through this dark time until I make the effort to do all of the things I know that I should, but accept that I am making progress as fast as I can while trying to resist a manic dash for the finish line that is likely to end up in a crash.

If nothing else, it is safe to conclude that John proved even the deepest despair can be a path to enlightenment. Through his personal triumph over spiritual pain, Saint John of the Cross was forced into an awareness more profound than all his intellect and learning could ever provide. His meditations and prayers may have brought him to ecstatic states, but in the end, it was his *Dark Night of the Soul* that defined Saint John of the Cross.

Francis of Assisi

The Prayer of Saint Francis

"O Lord, make me an instrument of Thy Peace!
Where there is hatred, let me sow love;
Where there is injury, pardon;
Where there is discord, harmony;
Where there is doubt, faith;
Where there is despair, hope;
Where there is darkness, light, and
Where there is sorrow, joy.
Oh Divine Master, grant that I may not
so much seek to be consoled as to console;
to be understood as to understand; to be loved
as to love; for it is in giving that we receive;
It is in pardoning that we are pardoned;
and it is in dying that we are born to Eternal Life."[1]

Saint Francis

1 Prayer attributed to St. Francis in 13th century, www.worldprayers.org

Love Conquers All

Francis of Assisi lived an unparalleled life of joy and love. His compassion for all people and all of Nature is represented in poetry, drawings, paintings and frescos around the world. Like the lives of the other saints, his early years did not predict the impact his life would have on the world.

Francis of Assisi had a very wise answer for every situation and person. He was consistent in his message and his actions throughout his life. Whether directed at nobility or beggars, his message was always "love."

Love is an unwavering truth of our humanity. Francis did not need theology or philosophy to explain it. His commitment to this truth meant constant right action.

For Francis to choose love in every situation meant that his actions had to demonstrate his love. He could not just think about love and do something else. For Francis, love was a verb. It meant taking the right action at every opportunity.

Italy In The Thirteenth Century

The 13th century was characterized by the urbanization of Europe, military expansion, and intellectual revival. The cities of antiquity had been clustered around the Mediterranean. By 1200 AD, the growing urban centers were in the middle of the continent, connected by roads or rivers.

France, England and Spain had developed into sovereign nations. Elsewhere in Europe, the Catholic church asserted its power over all the Christian world. The

Crusades were the military arm of the Church, expanding the empire into Egypt, Palestine and Northern Africa.

The Early Life of Francis

Francis was born in 1182, in the busy trading city of Assisi, in what is now Italy. The territory of Assisi occupies the northern part of the Umbrian valley, bounded by Mount Subasio and the hills that separate it from the Tiber Valley. It is a beautiful region, with rolling hills, vineyards, pastoral valleys and wide open clear sky.

Francis' father, Pietro Bernardone, was a wealthy textile merchant. Francis was raised in an environment of wealth, with many good friends and contacts that he gained from his father's business. Francis planned to follow him in his trade, although he also had dreams of being a troubadour or a knight. His mother, Pica, belonged to a noble family of Provence, France. He derived his name and his love of the Troubadours from this side of his heritage.

Although he showed little aptitude for school or business, he charmed everyone around him. He loved to sing and entertain his friends. He was always courteous, kind and cheerful.

Most of his friends came from the noble classes above his own class, but Francis was welcomed among them. No one loved pleasure more than Francis; he was smart, funny, sang merrily, delighted in fine clothes and had a dramatic flare. He soon became the favorite among the young nobles of Assisi, "the leader of the civil revels, the very king of frolic."[1]

In his father's business, it was Francis who attracted all the clients. It was Francis' good cheer, helpful attitude and quick wit that they enjoyed. He always extended a helping hand and had a "heart of gold." He was a great salesman, and his father's textile business thrived.[2]

There were countless times when Francis extended his aid to the poor so much that his father thought it endangered his business or hurt his profits. Francis would take off at a moment's notice to offer a beggar a cloak for the the cold, leaving the merchandise unattended. Once he left the shop in search of a woman beggar whom he had pushed aside when he was busy. He wandered the streets until he found her and gave her money. His attention to the suffering of others began long before he dedicated his life to the church.

Depression Transforms Francis

When Francis was 20, he and his friends joined the war in Perugia, not far from his home of Assisi. They were captured and held as prisoners of war for one year. Francis tried to keep everyone's spirits uplifted and optimistic. He entertained them by singing songs and telling stories. He was so intent on relieving the suffering of others that he never noticed his own. By the time of their release, Francis was nearing a complete collapse.

---

1 Robinson, Paschal, St. Francis of Assisi, Catholic Encyclopedia, 1909, Robert Appleton Company, N.Y., Vol.6, p.221, www.NewAdvent.org

2 Fulop-Miller, Rene, The Saints That Moved the World, Reprint ed. 1991, Ayer Co. Pub., N.H., p.159

A short time after arriving home, Francis became delirious and had to stay indoors in bed for several weeks. His nights were full of unexplained fevers, nightmares, visions and voices in his head. He never felt fully conscious or able to wake himself. He also never felt like he was sleeping. The only thing that brought him back to consciousness was the sunlight on his bed every morning.

Francis developed a love for the sun during this illness. His nights were so tortured that the rising sun brought him relief and joy. He began to get out of bed in the morning to greet the sun, and again in the evening to watch the last rays.[1]

As Francis slowly improved, he walked outside to be in the sunshine; at first he roamed to the end of his street, and eventually outside the walls of Assisi and into the countryside. His nights remained difficult. He would again fall into delirium and have fevers. As the sun rose and shone over the city, Francis experienced the light enveloping all the buildings and trees. As he walked in the countryside, he saw how the sunlight bathed everything in its glow. He began to experience ecstatic states of bliss and oneness with all of nature.

After the illness, Francis was more reflective. He spent time alone, walking in the countryside, waiting for those ecstatic states. He continued to go out with his friends and have parties at his house, but all the festivities of his nightlife were losing their charm. He was often distant and pensive in the company of his friends, and they began to tease him about being so distracted. They thought he was in love.

---

1 Fulop-Miller, Rene, *The Saints That Moved the World*, Reprint ed. 1991, Ayer Co. Pub., N.H., p.165

A Failed Crusade

Francis was looking for meaning and purpose. As invading German forces pushed toward Rome, Assisi put together a volunteer army to fight under the French knight, Walter of Brienne. Francis had a very prophetic dream and was filled with enthusiasm for the cause of saving his country and fighting in the army of the Pope.

He mounted his horse with all the gear of a Crusader and proudly joined the volunteers before they left the town of Assisi. He rode around and called out to his friends that he would come back as a great knight.

On his first night out, his illness returned with its fever and delirium. Francis was forced to stop and spend the night in the town of Spoleto.[1]

In that state between sleep and wakefulness, he heard voices and believed they were from God. The voices told him to return to Assisi; the war he would fight was not on the battlefield. When Francis mounted his horse the next morning, he thought the dreams were just his illness. He thought he headed out in the right direction to rejoin the others, but after a long days journey, he looked up and saw the gates of Assisi. Too tired with the fatigue of his fever and the long ride, he rode slowly into Assisi.

Francis was not met with compassion. The townspeople had only curses, scorn, laughter and taunts for him. He was humiliated. He had been so proud to ride off on his horse, and now had to wake every morning to his failure.

---

1 Jewett, Sophie, God's Troubadour, The Story of Saint Francis of Assisi, 1910, Thomas Y. Crowell Company, N.Y., www.catholicforum.com

Francis was confused and depressed. His friends had a difficult time cajoling him back to the parties and nightlife. Almost daily, he began to visit the little church of San Damiano, imploring God to make his purpose clear.

For a long time, Francis received no clues and no signs from God about what he should do. Then one night, in a state of half dreaming, he heard the voices again, "Go, Francis, and repair my house, which as you see is falling into ruin."[1]

Taking these words literally, Francis went to his father's warehouse and found some rolls of fabric that he could take to a local fair. He sold all of it. Then he sold his horse. He returned with the money to San Damiano and offered all of the money to begin rebuilding the church. The priest knew Pietro Bernardone well enough to wait until his return before accepting the donation.

Pietro Bernardone was a merchant and his son had taken valuable inventory. This was by far the most costly of Francis' escapades. His father was becoming more enraged with each incident and this turned out to be the last. He dragged his son before the bishop, who had power to make civil determinations at this time. Francis' father wanted his money back, and he wanted to disown Francis from the family fortunes before he could squander any more of it.

Francis made it easy for him. He returned all the money, stepped out of the clothes he was wearing, and told his father, "Hitherto I have called you my father on earth; henceforth I desire to say only, 'Our Father who art in

---

1 Robinson, Paschal, St. Francis of Assisi, Catholic Encyclopedia, 1909, Robert Appleton Company, N.Y., Vol.6, p.221, www.NewAdvent.org

Heaven.'"[1] Naked, Francis walked away from his father and out of town.

The Franciscan Friars

Francis had made his commitment to God by walking away from his worldly father. It surprised everyone, but for Francis it was the only logical thing to do. He took a few days to wander the countryside. He felt joy and freedom, not misery.

Returning to Assisi, Francis wore the simple, hooded robe of the peasants, with a rope tied around his waist for a belt. He began the restoration of San Damiano by walking the city begging for stones. Going out and retrieving stones, cutting them to fit, positioning them correctly and cementing them in place was tough work. It was a time of introspection for Francis. As he moved stones, he contemplated all that he had been through.

The work of repairing San Damiano strengthened Francis. His work became an ongoing meditation. He realized that every time he helped the poor or lifted a stone to the wall, he was doing God's work. He tried to imitate the simplicity of the life of Jesus. His interior life became confident and sure. It took over one year to rebuild the church, but when Francis finished, he knew how he wanted to proceed.

Francis started preaching in the region around Assisi. He called the people of the countryside to brotherly love. The people of Assisi had already stopped making fun of

---

1 Robinson, Paschal, St. Francis of Assisi, Catholic Encyclopedia, 1909, Robert Appleton Company, N.Y., Vol.6, p.221, www.NewAdvent.org

Francis. They began to admire his determination and commitment.

It did not take long before others volunteered to join him; a successful merchant was first, followed by a priest from Assisi. Francis brought his two companions to the cathedral at San Damiano. As was the custom, he randomly opened the Bible three times on the altar. Each time it opened, he read passages where Christ told His disciples to leave all things and follow Him. "This shall be our rule of life", exclaimed Francis, and led his companions to the public square, where they gave away all their belongings to the poor. They wore the rough, hooded robe of the peasants, like that of Francis. [1]

Francis wished to emulate Jesus in his gospel of peace and love. He did not want property to corrupt that purpose. He believed in the purity of the teachings and example of the life of Jesus. He rightfully observed that the Catholic church became corrupt through its accumulation of wealth.

When the number of his companions had increased to eleven, Francis wrote the first Rule of the Friars Minor. It was very short and simple. Francis asked that scholars and priests not try to interpret the Rule. "Just as the Lord helped me to state and write the Rules simply and plainly, so you must understand them simply and plainly without interpretation."[2]

---

1 Robinson, Paschal, St. Francis of Assisi, Catholic Encyclopedia, 1909, Robert Appleton Company, N.Y., Vol.6, p.221, www.NewAdvent.org

2 Fulop-Miller, Rene, The Saints That Moved the World, Reprint ed. 1991, Ayer Co. Pub., N.H., p. 270

One of his first followers was a scholar who "realized suddenly that salvation does not rest in man's knowledge of the things that are true, but in living and acting according to the truth."[1]

Francis always emphasized that the expressions of love and peace must be given freely. If people, animals, and nature felt his love, they would respond in kind.

Francis began preaching in fields and town squares. As Francis and his teachings gained in popularity, the priests invited him back to give sermons in their churches. His father now showed great pride in his son who attracted so many followers.

Lover Of Animals

Francis was known to speak with all kinds of animals. Birds greeted him and sang in chorus. Animals watched over him or followed him wherever he went. He was simply extending his radiant love to them. They understood they were in no danger with Francis.

One day, as Francis came into a village, the birds flew all around him and sang without stopping. When it came time for Francis to give his sermon, he realized no one would be able to hear him above the joyful songs of the birds. Looking up, he asked them to be quiet while he talked. "When he had blessed them with the sign of the cross, they sprang up, and singing songs of unspeakable

---

1 Ibid., p.196

sweetness, away they streamed in a great cross to the four quarters of heaven."[1]

In one town, Francis encountered a hunting party on the way to track and kill a wolf that was raiding the town's livestock. Francis asked to go along. When the wolf was spotted in a field, Francis asked the men to let him go out alone and talk to the wolf. The hunting party was very afraid of the wolf, but with gentle reassurances, Francis persuaded them to let him try.

To their surprise, the wolf did not run away or attack. The wolf licked Francis' feet and bowed down to him. Francis knelt in the snow and spoke with the wolf, which became playful and puppy-like. Francis turned and walked back toward the hunting party with the wolf dutifully at his heels.

The men stood in awe and fear until they could see that his love had transformed the "beast" inside of the wolf. Francis asked the men to let the wolf into the city and care for it. He promised them this wolf would not hunt again. The wolf became a favorite of the village and the people cared for him until he died. They erected a statue of Francis with the wolf in the town square. It was a reminder of his lesson that even something feared is deserving of love.

Beggars and Bandits

One evening when he arrived back at the monastery, Brother Angelo excitedly told Francis how he had chased off three highway robbers that had come begging for some

---

1 Canton, William, A Child's Book of Saints, The Little Bedesman of Christ, 1906, E.P. Dutton & Co., N.Y., www.gutenberg.org

bread. The villagers had cornered the bandits in the woods for weeks, and were starving them out. Angelo declared that the men were brazen and impudent to come to the monastery for food.

Francis was more surprised by Angelo's reaction to the bandits than anything else. How could his own disciple act without love and compassion? Francis sent Angelo to find the bandits, accompanied with bread and wine from the monastery table. He asked Angelo to beg their forgiveness in Francis' name, and invite the bandits to return to the monastery.

When Francis brought them into the monastery he talked to them with brotherly love. There was no tone of admonishment or judgment in his voice. Brother Angelo was humbled by the boundless heart of Francis and the strength of his actions.

Francis found no need for punishment in changing human hearts. "Severity induces fear; punishment deepens the abyss of loneliness; and only brotherly love can unite all of creation as one great family of God."[1] The bandits were able to see the good in themselves because that is what Francis saw in them.

Pilgrim Of Peace

Francis went to the Holy Land in 1221. He did not go as a Crusader, as he idealized in his youth, but as a peacemaker.

---

1 Fulop-Miller, Rene, The Saints That Moved the World, Reprint ed. 1991, Ayer Co. Pub., N.H., p. 246

Francis first spoke to the Crusaders in their camps at the Port of Damietta, Egypt. He was dismayed at the Crusader's lust for blood and the treasure they were stealing. He told them that it was their own evil behavior, not the Muslims, that kept them out of the Holy Land. He begged that they not enter the Holy Land until they had purified their souls. "It is greed and hatred that keeps you from the Holy Land... If you wear a cross on your armor, wear it also in your heart... Swords win blood, but love wins souls."[1]

Against passionate pleas for common sense, Francis left the Crusaders encampment at Damietta and set out for the Muslim camp. As when Anthony walked unharmed through the streets of Alexandria during the Christian persecutions, Francis walked unharmed all the way to the tents of the Muslim leader.

Francis asked permission to speak with Malik al Kamil. He was politely received and invited inside. The two men spoke in French and understood one another. They expressed their love for Mohammed or Jesus Christ, respectively, and neither could be persuaded to renounce his own faith. The meeting ended with graciousness and courtesy.

Francis was allowed to tour the Holy Land, protected by the Muslim guards of Malik al Kamil. By his love, understanding, peaceful words, and actions, he gained entry to all the holy places of pilgrimage in the middle of war.[2]

---

1 Fulop-Miller, Rene, The Saints That Moved the World, Reprint ed. 1991, Ayer Co. Pub., N.H., p.246

2 Fulop-Miller, Rene, The Saints That Moved the World, Reprint ed. 1991, Ayer Co. Pub., N.H., p.245

Meanwhile in Damietta, the Muslim and Christian armys took up the bloody battle where thousands were killed. Francis understood he could not change the course of their actions. They were not going to listen to him.

Francis' later years

Francis had always insisted that the Franciscan Friars abstain from owning property. He never believed it was necessary to maintain an organization. His ideal was that the Franciscans remain forever as a band of wandering minstrels for God.

In the time since Francis had begun teaching, he had attracted thousands of followers. Men and women, monastics, and entire families had followed his ideals. Among the brothers, there were many who longed to build beautiful churches and libraries. Others wished to organize and administrate, creating structure for the Franciscan Order.

By the time Francis returned from Egypt, he found an entire organization had been created in his absence. Mansions had been accepted as gifts to be used for libraries and monasteries.

A new home had just been donated to the Franciscans in Bologna. The brothers were filled with excitement, planning a festive opening ceremony. When Francis arrived, he was dismayed at the luxurious mansion. He asked them what had become of their vows of poverty. His friars could not calm him, and he walked out on the ceremony.[1]

---

1 Fulop-Miller, Rene, The Saints That Moved the World, Reprint ed. 1991, Ayer Co. Pub., N.H., p.254

Shortly after this, he resigned from the administrative duties and his leadership of the organization. Initially, one of Francis' most loved and devoted brothers, Pietro dei Cattani, took leadership, but Pietro only lived for a few more months.

Brother Elias and Cardinal Ugolino took control of the Franciscan order and requested that Francis rewrite "The Rule." They intended to ease the restrictions, making it easier to follow. Francis tried to stop them, but he found it very difficult. Brother Elias and Cardinal Ugolino were both completely devoted to the Franciscan order and wanted to see it survive and flourish. For Francis, it was a losing battle.

Many of Francis' most loyal brothers protested that he had let his power slip away. "I am not my brother's keeper" was all that the disheartened saint could answer. He vowed that the only remedy was to teach through his example.[1]

Francis did not work officially within the Franciscan Brotherhood again. He led by his example, which had always been his most powerful tool. He continued to transform hearts, and light the way for those who would listen.

Peace, Joy and Love

Francis contracted a severe eye inflammation while he was in Egypt. No one in Italy could cure it, and he suffered with it until his death. When it began to deteriorate, he had to stay inside in the dark because the daylight was so painful for him. He could only go outside at night.

---

1 Ibid., p.258

This was the man who adored being out in the sunlight, enjoying flowers, and walking with the songs of birds. Although this condition would have been miserable for anyone else; Francis was the exception. Ever the optimist, and the one to point out the good side of any situation, Francis now exalted the moon and stars, the night birds, and the quiet breezes of the evening.

The doctors tried every remedy, but failed to find a cure for his pain, or for any of the other symptoms. He had to be attended to 24 hours a day by doctors, brothers, and nuns. They all loved Francis deeply and worried over his worsening condition. Even in his severe pain and illness, Francis sang to them and made them laugh.[1]

As he lay near death, he offered up his life of peace to heal one last conflict. The bishop and the municipal pastor of Assisi were locked in a bitter dispute. Using his own illness as a pretext, he asked each of them to appear at his side at a particular hour. They both arrived not expecting the presence of the other.

Francis sang his "Canticle to Brother Sun" with his two disciples. As the singing came to an end, Francis added another stanza, "Blessed are they that keep themselves in peace." The two gentlemen were so moved by the moment that they begged forgiveness of Francis and of each other, and were reconciled.[2]

The final stanza of the "Canticle to Brother Sun" welcomes Sister Death. Francis could be heard singing until

---

1 Fulop-Miller, Rene, The Saints That Moved the World, Reprint ed. 1991, Ayer Co. Pub., N.H., p.263

2 Fulop-Miller, Rene, The Saints That Moved the World, Reprint ed. 1991, Ayer Co. Pub., N.H., p.268

almost his final hour. At his death, birds are said to have flown into the air circling and singing their praise.

Francis died in 1226 and was canonized by Pope Gregory IX in 1228. The statue of the little man in the brown robe, saint of love and compassion, surrounded by doves of peace, is known throughout the world.

Lessons of Saint Francis

Although Saint Francis also had depression as a central part of his change into a saint, I have included his story because he is the greatest example of how we should act. Saint Francis is revered because he chose to act perfectly in all situations. If we could follow his example in even minor ways, the world would be a much better place.

Many followers of both western and eastern philosophies speak of the duality of the world. This duality is seen by many to be the work of the devil, or to the eastern world, delusion. Disease and health, pain and pleasure, loss and gain—these are all examples of the opposites that hold together our false reality.[1]

I often hear the idea that once we attain enlightenment, we live in bliss. If bliss is defined as great joy, is that just one side of duality? I think something may have been lost in the translation of the original meaning.

If enlightenment brings bliss, why were the saints in this book suffering until the end? I think it is because bliss does not mean happy, it means acceptance that everything is part of the same oneness: as I noted in the chapter *The Art of*

---

1 Paramahansa Yogananda, *Aurobiography of a Yogi*, 1993, Self Realization Fellowship, L.A., p.486

Seeing Depression, "It's all milk." Depression is just as much a part of bliss as any other state. Peace, love, and joy are naturally felt, even when you are also experiencing great pain. If you read what Saint Teresa, Saint John of the Cross, or Saint Francis had to say, it will become clear: bliss is not the opposite of duality, it includes duality as a subset.

Picture two small circles next to each other. One is pleasure and the other is pain. The common concept is that we get to a point that is outside of them both and move to another circle where there is only peace, love, and joy. Bliss is incorrectly thought of as beyond the duality, a place where pleasure and pain do not exist.

Now picture a larger circle with the pleasure and pain inside of it. Picture it with all conditions inside of it: pleasure, pain, gain, loss, happiness, sadness, health, illness, etc. If you focus on the big circle, you are in bliss, even though you are still experiencing some of the elements inside. If you lose the perspective of the big circle, you feel only the small circles, and the pain seems more intense.

Some people think that the problem is that we have wrong thinking. They propose that we catch ourselves thinking sad thoughts and replace them with happy thoughts, as if that is going to change the picture. It is the same as focusing on the two small circles. We will never fully understand our condition until we begin to focus on the big circle and find meaning in our experiences. As long as you think that sad thoughts are an illness you will not find the advantage of your condition.

The example of our saints is that they got to a point that they were in the same state of oneness no matter what happened to their body or mind. Saint Francis was in incredible pain at the end of his life, yet had the ability to keep focused on the big picture. It is not that he was somehow separate from his experiences; he experienced them just as you and I would. But since he was focusing on the big picture, he was in bliss. Bliss is the state that is not affected by the duality.

As our saints grew in understanding, they still experienced the pain, but from the perspective of bliss it did not affect them as much. That is why Saint Teresa said: "All these illnesses now bother me so little that I am often glad, thinking the Lord is served by something."[1]

It takes the perspective of extreme pain for some of us to see the truth of bliss. The *Depression Advantage* is that we have the chance to understand something that few ever will.

---

1 Teresa of Avila: Mystical Writings, ed. Tessa Bielecki, 1999, Crossword Publishing Company, NY. p.119

Our Advantage Over The Saints

It may sound crazy, but we actually do have several advantages that the saints did not.

They Have Already Shown The Way

The saints were on their own. They had to navigate the path with no guide or understanding. They had nothing but faith to carry them through their hardships.

Don't underestimate faith. It may be the strongest tool we have to get through when times get really tough. But faith doesn't have to be a religious thing. After reading about the saints, you should at least have faith in the fact that someone else was able to overcome issues similar, if not worse, than our own.

Although we may not care to follow their paths, the lives of the saints can at least give us guidance. How can we follow their example? Is there anything that worked for them that might work for us?

The saints didn't just set examples for us, they shared what they learned and tried to show the way to others. Saint

Teresa and Saint John of the Cross even wrote directions! If we want to change our lives, there is no greater proof of what is possible than the examples and teachings of the saints.

We Have Tools They Never Had

The saints in this book lived hundreds of years ago. Back then, there was no research into how the brain functions or how various factors contributed to their conditions. Science has come a long way in understanding what is happening and what we can do to manage our condition.

The knowledge that mankind has gained gives us an incredible advantage. Modern medicine has figured out so much that it would seem like a miracle to anyone from even 100 years ago. Through brain research, genetics, modern psychology, and the synthesis of knowledge from cultures across the globe, we stand at the crossroads of a new paradigm of mental health. I believe it is one that will change mental illness into an advantage for everyone. As we learn more about how the mind operates, we will begin to make advancements that will change the world.

The most recent advancements in medication are an advantage that we might take for granted. Our generation has a very powerful arsenal in medications that have been developed in the last 20 years. These drugs can give us control over the extremes of our mood and behavior. Used properly, they can keep us from suffering from our condition.

The understanding of psychology has created therapies that are helping millions of people lessen the pain and develop skills. A professional therapist is a major advantage over toughing it out in a cave.

Technology has produced tools that are amazing. From simple tools like light therapy to make up for seasonal depression, to biofeedback that helps us become more aware, we have tools that can make a huge difference in our lives.

There are so many more tools that it would become a laundry list just to mention them all. Suffice it to say that we have a major advantage over the saints because of the knowledge to which we have access.

We Don't Have To Suffer To Succeed

There are plenty of saints that got there without living the extreme lives of those in this book. Many have made their goal without the suffering. When you study the lives of saints, you will find that there are as many paths to get there as there are saints. Suffering is not a prerequisite. I used the examples in this book to demonstrate that it is possible no matter how bad we feel.

We can use our condition as an opportunity to follow in their footsteps. We can learn from their experiences and follow their advice. Beginning now, you can combine their advice with the help of your team and your own hard work to change yourself. A great therapist can help us to gain the insights without the need to go to such extremes.

We Don't Have To Be Depressed Again

When you get to the point that you can safely look back, you can learn from your past conditions. I can remember past depressions as if they are happening right now. You can too. Many of us have already been to states comparable to those of the saints. We can learn just as well from the safety of a stable condition as we can from going there again.

The same lessons are in our memory as in our future. Once we learn the lessons, the future episodes will have less pain because of our change in perception. We may even find that they never happen again, or at least not with the same intensity.

Long before we get to sainthood, we develop understanding that lessens the pain. The saints in this book all talked about having the same experiences as before, but seeing them in a completely different way. If you look back at your own life, you can see what once seemed impossibly painful is not really that hard anymore. Imagine looking back on your worst episodes with the understanding that Saint Teresa developed.

Our Condition Demands Introspection And Change

The potential to learn from our pain is the same advantage the saints had, but when you begin to see the opportunity, you will find that this is our advantage over everyone else. "Normal" people can go about the rest of their lives pretending everything is fine; we cannot. We are faced with a condition that grabs our attention and will kill us if we do not take action and turn it into our advantage.

You can see it as a curse, or choose to see it as an advantage. Seeing it as a curse will consign you to a life of hell that may be cut short; seeing it as an advantage can give you the insight to use every tool at your disposal to turn your life into the potential that you have. The choice is yours.

How Do You Get There?

The Concepts Of The Bipolar In Order Workshops

It is important to view any mental condition as having a combination of both good and bad aspects. When we see the whole picture, we can accept the possibility that our condition has a range from illness to advantage.

It is an illness when it is ruining your life, and it is totally out of your control. It is a disorder when it is not necessarily ruining your life, but it is having a negative impact on your life. It is a vulnerability when a chance exists that it might cause you to act up and do some bad things. It is an advantage when you finally figure out how to take the traits and turn them into something that helps you to grow.

There are clear steps we can follow that will help us to turn our condition into an advantage; Acceptance, Introspection, Focus, Creating A Business Plan For Success, Getting Help, and Your Own Hard Work.

Acceptance

Acceptance is the first step. We will never get anywhere until we recognize the importance of it. Acceptance means we are no longer in denial, but are willing to see our condition for what it really is. We need to accept the fact that we have this condition and it is not going away on its own. We cannot just mask it; we need to accept the good and bad traits that we have. Until we do, it is difficult for others to help us, and it is impossible for us to help ourselves.

Parents come to me all the time, frustrated that they can't make a difference: "What can I do? My son refuses to accept the fact that he has this. What are our choices?" In conferences filled with both experts and consumers, no one really has an answer. You can lock them up for a few days but they will never trust you again. Until they come to acceptance, they will never make the effort to change. I wish I had an answer, but we all share the same frustration on this issue.

In our one day workshop, we break into small groups for this exercise:

Each person tells the others in the small group what acceptance means and why it is an important first step. Once each person shares his or her feelings, they work out a consensus definition. This takes a long time to work through, but having to express something to others is one of the best ways to become clear about it yourself. We compare all of the group definitions, and have a discussion about what we have learned. The commonality of ideas in all of the workshops I have facilitated is amazing.

Acceptance definitions from the workshop:

• It is the foundation for the building blocks that we need to get better.

• It is the beginning of taking back control of our lives.

• It is the comfort and understanding of who we are and where we are. It is exerting some control to become a better person, yet allowing for mistakes. It is taking responsibility for our actions, and not succumbing to self pity.

• It is being fully apprised, aware, and accountable, while being at peace with ourselves. It is being able to be ourselves. It is being open to the past and present without judgment.

• It is being self aware, being able to love ourselves as a whole, unconditionally. It is living with the consequences, both positive and negative of our actions. It is being willing to change habits, tendencies, and behaviors. It is knowing that we can only begin to accept others, by accepting ourselves. It is a key component to lifting relationships to a new level.

• It is learning how to grow. It is understanding what is happening. It is continuing our learning, then applying the knowledge through practice. It is knowing that we will not get it right the first time, but must keep practicing.

• It is being honest about what we are experiencing, what we have done, and what we have chosen, while loving ourselves at the same time.

• It is accepting people around us with their expectations or preconceived ideas about who we can become.

Acceptance is not surrender. Acceptance means to love ourselves for who we are right now, while striving to become someone we can love even more tomorrow. A point that is brought up in every workshop is that personal growth and the desire to change is a central component of both acceptance and forgiveness. We all agree that we have to come to acceptance before we can begin to change anything about our condition, our circumstances, and our relationships.

We need to work on acceptance for the rest of our lives. The acceptance we may have today is often conditioned on expectations that we are going to improve. When a few months go by, and we have not made the progress we were hoping for, we will need to accept that too. Acceptance is something that happens in the moment. We all need to accept our circumstances, other people, and ourselves, every moment of every day.

Introspection

How many of us, before we go out in public, look in the mirror, make sure our hair looks nice, and that we are dressed well? Why do we do that? Is it because we want to be attractive to other people? How many of us look into how we are thinking and acting before we go out?

I ask those questions at every talk that I give. Almost everybody raises their hand about grooming, but when I ask about thoughts and actions, very few count that among their daily habits. I counted six people out of 650 once, and often count zero in a crowd. It impresses upon me how little we have thought about it as a society.

If we want to be attractive to everybody, why do we take our ugly habits out there and ruin everything? Shouldn't we be looking at our inside, and not be so obsessed about our outward appearance? St. Francis didn't care how he looked on the outside. Although outwardly he was not a handsome man, he was one of the most attractive people that ever lived. It was the way he acted that caught others' attention. If we learn how to change our behaviors, we can become someone truly attractive to the world.

Introspection is the examination or observation of one's own mental and emotional processes. It is the practice of looking into the mirror of our thoughts and actions. The practice I teach in the one day workshop only takes two minutes a day and provides remarkable benefits. The process allows our subconscious mind to monitor our thoughts, our triggers, and our actions. It allows us to see our progress.

Introspection relies on acceptance. It is important that we can accept ourselves each time we practice introspection. We must be willing to honestly look at ourselves every day.

Our therapists, family and friends, clergy, teachers, and even strangers see things about us that we do not. If we are willing to notice the way other people respond to us, we will get definite clues about how we are really behaving. By learning to see ourselves as others see us, we can begin to see ourselves for who we really are, instead of who we delude ourselves into thinking we are.

Introspection is the most important thing we will ever do. We **will not** do anything about our condition unless we accept it, but we **cannot** do anything about it without introspection. How are we going to change ourselves, or even know what to change, without a clear understanding of what we are working with?

In *The Bipolar Advantage,* there is a chapter about introspection based on the exercise we do in the one day workshop. *The Bipolar In Order Workbook* has thorough explanations of introspection. The two day workshop has deep introspection as the primary activity. It includes a deep look at our fears, relationships, mental, physical, emotional, and spiritual lives, as well as career and financial goals.

I can't stress enough the importance of some kind of introspection practice. If you take just one thing away from this book, please make it the start of a lifetime habit of introspection. It is the most important step any of us will ever take.

Focus

The root cause of all mental conditions can be traced to our inability to control our own minds. You can't even introspect unless you develop the ability to focus on the task.

During every workshop, we create lists of good and bad traits that people with mental conditions live with everyday. Near the top of that list is always: "My mind goes all over the place, it races, and is out of my control." It is undeniable that controlling our mind is our biggest problem. There are those who doubt that the mind can be brought under control, but I never said it was easy. It is the hardest challenge we will ever face.

A good way to start is to learn to brainstorm. In the one day workshop, I teach the science behind how the mind can take advantage of brainstorming, giving concrete methods to do that. This is detailed in *The Bipolar Advantage* and *The Bipolar In Order Workbook*, so I don't want to repeat it too much here.

Simple version: write down everything you can think of about a topic for three minutes. Most of us with racing minds will find we are naturally gifted at brainstorming. For us, the most important part of the exercise is not that we learn to brainstorm; it is actually that we learn to tell our mind to stop on our command.

At the end of three minutes, count up how many items you wrote down. You are now focusing on the counting instead of the flow of ideas. You have told your brain to switch off the racing thoughts and change functions. By practicing this every day, we slowly learn how to stop our mind from racing.

Are racing thoughts a good or a bad thing? They are a horrible thing when they are out of your control, but an asset once you learn to control them.

We have minds that are on fire so often, and are so out of control, that we need stronger methods than just learning how to stop them in controlled circumstances.

I have been practicing a stronger method my whole life. I learned how to focus the mind on one thing, blocking out all other thoughts and sensations. You can develop this skill too. The object of focus can be your breath, a candle, or an idea; it really doesn't matter what it is.

The first time you sit down for three minutes and decide you are going to focus, the same thing will happen to you that happens to everyone else. You set your watch, and at the end of three minutes, you realize you thought about your object of focus only at the very beginning, and after that your mind went all over the place. That is normal and experienced by everyone in the beginning.

After a few weeks of daily practice, you start to realize that you are able to return to the point of focus over and over again. After a few months of practicing every day, you can focus on one thing for a couple of minutes at a time. You have begun to succeed in training your mind.

It takes about six months of daily practice until you establish control. When you find your thoughts racing, stop and decide: "Hey, my mind is racing—**focus**," and you will find you have the power to do it.

The reason Tiger Woods is so good is because he trained his mind to focus on what he is doing and nothing else. He blocks out all distractions and all of the thoughts that say he is going to screw up. He says to himself "I am focusing on doing it right and I have practiced over and over again." When you talk to people who are successful at anything, they will tell you that the ability to focus is the key to success. Why don't we practice it? Three minutes a day is all that it takes to prove to yourself that it works.

The mind can be brought under control, but we have to do the hard work it takes to accomplish it. We have to make consistent effort over a long period to see results. It doesn't happen overnight, so we have to stick with it. When you take the cast off of a broken limb, you have to do physical therapy and exercise your muscles in order to make them powerful enough to function again. We need to do the same thing with our minds: exercise them in ways that will make them stronger. There are countless ways we can stimulate our minds to grow; focus is the number one exercise.

Business Plan For Success

Turning mental conditions like bipolar and depression into an advantage requires a real plan to succeed. There have to be clear, well defined goals. We can figure out a plan that will get us there - if we are sure what "there" means.

Every successful business follows a plan. Companies traded on the stock market must have a written plan and announce every three months how they are doing. Those that are successful are good at setting reasonable and achievable goals, and staying on track to achieve them.

The secret is to be able to change the plan according to the circumstances. If an outside influence changes, the best companies are able to adapt their plans to stay competitive. We must learn to do the same with our life plans. A life plan, of course, is not about making money as much as getting your life to work for you.

At our one day workshop, I take the hardest topic there is. During the last hour of the workshop, I say: "Let's take depression and turn it into an advantage." We do an example together, building a plan that says we are going to go from seeing depression as the worst thing in our lives to seeing depression as an advantage.

By then, I have already told my story of how I have turned rage into an advantage over the course of eight years. This includes a definition of what an advantage means. In the case of rage, it means that I no longer rage at anyone, I understand it at a much deeper level than practically anyone, and I have the ability to help other people control their rage. Some people would say that I have "mastered" rage.

In the case of depression, I let the workshop members define what requirements must be met to claim depression as an advantage. This process makes it their definition, not mine. I only interject when they try to set an unreasonable definition (like never to be depressed again).

A recent group came up with the following list:

• Come to acceptance.

• No suicide risk. Suicide prevention plan in place.

• Ability to help others deal with depression.

• Understand the levels and components of depression.

• Active in advocacy for people with depression.

• Feel more in control during and getting out of depression.

• Extended range - able to handle deeper depressions.

• Finding lessons.

• No decline in housekeeping due to depression.

Another group came up with a similar but unique list:

- Acceptance

- No more fear or risk of suicide

- Less time below level 4

- Find lessons

- Better understanding

- Help depressed people

- Ability to see benefits

Every workshop group creates a different list of what it would take to claim depression as an advantage. We work on this list until everyone agrees that if these criteria are met, we could realistically claim that we have turned depression from something on our bad list to an advantage.

Once we have agreement of what criteria needs to be met, we then create a "business plan" timeline to get there. We all hope that we can make it in five years and accept that we may not. Working with five years as the goal, we write down milestones that need to be achieved in order to know we are on track for success. Once again, this is a personal list that is different for each group. The group that made the first criteria above created the following timeline:

Tomorrow

- Review today's lessons

- Do three minutes of meditation

- Start working on acceptance

• Buy two books about depression

One Month

• Write a list of positives

• Five minutes of daily meditation

• Introspection questions well thought out

• Daily introspection started

• Started reading a book about depression

• Found a good therapist

Six Months

• Ten minutes of daily meditation

• Have developed clear descriptions of depressed states

• Written plans for handling crisis

• Finished reading one book and started another

• Talked to someone with depression, and helped them

• Relationship with therapist developed

One year

• Twenty minutes of daily meditation

• Advocacy for people with depression

• Some form of self-expression of what I have learned

• Read second book about depression

• Written list of causes of depression

• Definition of various levels of depression

• Read biographies of famous depressed people

Two Years

• Twenty minutes of meditation twice a day

• Lessons discovered

• Starting to gain control while getting in and out of depression

• Ability to handle deeper states without fear of suicide

• Wrote two articles about depression

• Refined list of causes

• Better functioning while depressed

• Running support group

There are still many things left to do, but there are three more years to go. This is not a complete plan, nor is it a prescription for everyone - it's just enough to get everyone thinking in terms of making small steps that are achievable. It is important to have clear objectives that are not going to be too hard to achieve. Once an objective is achieved, it can be built upon.

Take, for example, meditation as a habit to develop. Note that only three minutes a day for the first month leads to five minutes in the next month, ten minutes in six months, twenty minutes in a year, and only after two years does it ramp up to twenty minutes twice a day.

Too often people take on too much and do not achieve it. If you try twenty minutes of meditation, twice a day, from day one, you probably will not keep up the habit. If you work up slowly, the habit will get stronger as you feel the benefits, and you will be more likely to keep it up.

Someone inevitably asks, "What about the other things on the list that need changing?" A remarkable result of this exercise is that the path outlined will work for any part of the condition they would like to master - depression, rage, anger, impatience, etc. If I came right out and said it, the realization would not sink in, but the fact that they built the process and asked themselves, "What about the other things on the list? What steps can we take to master them?" creates a breakthrough. The same path outlined works for every issue.

Having taken the steps in my own effort to turn rage into an advantage, I have already developed the tools necessary to apply them to other traits I intend to master. Once success is achieved in turning one trait into an advantage, it is much easier to do it again and again. With each success, our ability to change the next item becomes easier and takes less time. Eventually, we should be able to master our condition and turn every trait to our advantage.

Every person so far has said: "Yes, I could do that." Personally, I see this as amazing. People walk in saying depression is the worst thing ever, and they walk out, six hours later, believing they can change it. I think the fact that they even accept the possibility is a huge change. It is possible to turn any mental condition into an advantage instead of a disadvantage, but we have to take action.

In our two day workshop, we each build our own personal plan for success that includes all of the aspects of our lives that we want to change. We end up with a clear, achievable plan that when followed leads to a much better life.

Get Help

We cannot do it alone. One of our greatest challenges is to communicate openly and honestly with our team, and they need to communicate openly and honestly with us. It is important to get beyond stigma and fear with everyone on our team.

Your Doctor

Your doctor has a critical role to play. By doctor I mean a psychiatrist, not just a general practitioner. They are the experts on how medications work, which ones to give, and how much of each is the best dosage for your current circumstances.

What I am proposing in this book is a paradigm shift for many doctors. If you are going to turn your condition into an advantage, you must find a doctor who believes in the possibility. A doctor who thinks that you have an illness that needs to be medicated into submission will prescribe too much medicine and keep you in the zero range, which will not work. You should be looking for a psychiatrist who views their responsibility as finding the least amount of medication possible to have the desired effect.

My doctor's role isn't to narrow my range of moods and experience down to zero. His role is to help me figure out the medication that allows me to function in a range that works for me. If my doctor helps me to find the right dosage, I can use my medication as the tool that it was meant to be.

Your Therapist

Your therapist is often a different person than the psychiatrist who prescribes medication. The therapist has to be your coach, guide, counselor, educator, and help you to see the things that you can't. Helping you to realize what is going on is a critical role that they are professionally trained to do.

A good therapist is the key to our making the changes necessary to create a better life. They have seen and helped many people in our situation, and have tremendous insight into what works and what doesn't. A healthy balance between receiving support and receiving candid feedback is crucial for success in all forms of inner work. It really helps to have a professional with an objective viewpoint on your team.

A list of therapists who believe in our concepts can be found at the Bipolar Advantage website[1]. They still practice with the same techniques, but have made the huge paradigm shift from focusing on illness to focusing on turning it into an advantage. If your therapist doesn't believe that you can turn your mental condition into an advantage, how is he or she going to help you get there?

All of our main concepts are covered by a good therapist: helping us to see the whole picture, acceptance,

---

1 http://www.bipolaradvantage.com

introspection and creating a clear path to success. They are not always trained in the practice of meditation or focus, but the best ones are. Bringing your plan to your therapist allows you to receive important feedback and help in making the adjustments necessary to achieve it.

Yourself

Our responsibility is to communicate what is working, what is not, and where we need help. We have to start telling the complete truth if our team is going to be able to help us. They can't help us if we don't communicate honestly. Otherwise, they are treating some fantasy person we made up, instead of treating us.

Our therapists might be our coaches, but we are the quarterback; we have to do the things they suggest, and use the information they helped us to learn. We can't just talk about the concepts, we have to live them. Everybody else can help, but it is our job to turn our lives around.

Your Family And Friends

In the scene at the train station in "The Hours,"[1] Virginia Woolf reminds her husband that she is a sovereign human being and ultimately, the choice of her destiny must be hers alone. This is the responsibility that each person with a mental condition must accept, and friends and family members must live with. However, the only way to thrive is to include your family and friends in your life.

---

1 "The Hours," Paramount Pictures, 2003, Directed by Stephen Daldry, written by Michael Cunningham (novel), David Hare, screenplay

Family and friends have a critical role to play, because they are there with us. We can lie to our therapists, but we can't lie to our family; they see it.

Unfortunately, sometimes this closeness can make things worse. Most often from lack of training, they provoke us when we are at our worst. When we are starting to lose control, they say: "You're losing it, you're losing it! Did you take your drugs today?" They start an argument with us, because they are afraid and don't have a better way to show concern. I think we have all experienced these situations.

I promise, you will never win an argument with a person with a mental condition when they are having an episode. It is not possible. But when we calm down later, you can find a way to communicate with us. We do want our relationships to work.

We all need to work on when it is appropriate to communicate and how to communicate more effectively. There are good books on communication and conflict resolution. Both sides should read them. Along with commitment; deep, sincere, and open communication will be what saves most relationships.

It is important to look at the big picture. Try to remember the improvements more than the setbacks, and emphasize progress and support instead of recrimination and frustration. Avoid perpetuating conflicts by expecting perfection in others. In our closest relationships, we must constantly practice acceptance and reestablishing trust.

Realize that everyday is a new opportunity to establish better relationships. Family members need to acknowledge our growth with deeper trust in us. Positive feedback, encouragement, and gratitude will go a long way between those with mental conditions and their family and friends.

Your Clergy

Duke University did a study that counted up how many hours clergy are spending with those who have mental conditions, versus how many hours professional therapists are spending.[1] They found out that the clergy in the U.S. are cumulatively spending more time counseling than all of the therapists combined. Unfortunately, the clergy do not have the same level of training. An increasing number of seminaries are offering courses in psychology, however, and pastors are more likely than ever to refer congregation members to professional therapists.[2]

My spiritual counselor taught me to quit calling it an illness and call it a condition. He changed my way of looking at it. A condition means it has both good and bad parts to it. It is not all horrible. We have to quit looking at it as a deficit-based illness and start looking at it as an opportunity for growth.

Those Of Us Who Have Been There

Last, but not least, those who have been there have a responsibility to help others in any way we can: empathy, assurance, and showing them that it is possible by our own

1 Buckholtz, Alison:"In Times of Trouble, Growing Numbers of People Take Comfort in Faith-Based Therapy"; Special to The Washington Post, Tuesday, December 6, 2005; Page HE04

2 Brinton, Henry, G., A Meeting in the Mind; Science and Faith Join Forces on Mental Illness., Washington Post, Sunday, June 12, 2005; p., B03

actions. Changing ourselves is our number one responsibility. If we can improve our condition, and turn it to an advantage, it is setting an example for other people to believe it is possible to do it themselves. Only by example can we show others a pathway to get there.

Your Own Hard Work

Doing the hard work to get a handle on this condition is the hardest thing you will ever do, except for one thing - not doing it. Because if we don't do it, we are going to suffer needlessly; we might even end our life early because we didn't try to improve our chances for success.

We Are The X-Men

You Have More Power Than You Can Imagine

I remember being a big fan of the TV show *The Incredible Hulk*[1] when I was a kid, and the *The Hulk*[2], *Spider-Man*[3], *Fantastic Four*[4], and the *X-Men*[5] series as movies when they came out. I always thought they portrayed mental illness in a quirky way, but I never realized the significance they had for me until recently. It was in watching the latest episode in the X-men series, *X-Men: The Last Stand*,[6] that it all came together for me. **We are the X-Men.**

---

1 "The Incredible Hulk" TV Series, 1978-1982, CBS, based on a character created by Stan Lee and Jack Kirby.

2 "The Hulk," Universal Pictures, 2003. Written by Michael France, John Turman and James Schamus.

3 "Spider Man," 2003, Columbia Pictures, written by David Koepp based on a character created by Stan Lee and Jack Kirby.

4 "The Fantastic Four," 2005, Twentieth Century-Fox Film Corporation,written by Mark Frost and Michael France.

5 "X-Men, The Last Stand," 2006, Twentieth Century-Fox Film Corporation, written by Simon Kinberg and Zak Penn

6 Ibid.

Stan Lee and the creators of all of those characters have shown uncanny insight into the nature of our condition and our struggles. All of their characters have special powers. They also have weird quirks and idiosyncrasies. Most of all, they struggle with their powers and their inability to handle them.

In watching *X-Men: The Last Stand*, I noticed several characters with whom I could relate. They wanted to live a "normal" life and could not see the benefit of a power that they could not control. They were subjected to overwhelming pressure to get "cured" of their disease, and many succumbed to the promise of a "normal" life.

Many fought to see the possibilities in harnessing their powers for good. As they gained the ability to handle their unique gifts, they found that they could control their super powers and turn them into an advantage.

As I struggle with my condition, I have learned that even some of the powers that had no apparent benefit were a source of great strength. I now see that my "super powers" give me the ability to do things a "normal" being couldn't even fathom. I also see that my lack of ability to harness them and keep them under control has brought me dangerously close to my own death.

Like the characters of Stan Lee's invention, I too would have done anything to become "normal," but in the end chose to engage in the ultimate battle: learning to get my powers under control to harness them for good.

The greatest power of all is my ability to go into such deep depression that I can gain insights into the true meaning of life. It helps me to find meaning and purpose beyond just surviving another day, and helps me to appreciate life for all of its richness. The ability to go from the depths of depression to the highs of mania has given my life a richness that I would never give up.

Of course, with those powers comes the struggle against them and our inability to harness them for good. In the end, we have no choice but to get them under control with any means available, including medications, therapy, and our own hard work. However, many choose to give up on the effort to harness our powers, for fear that we will never gain sufficient control over them.

The problem is not that we are mentally ill; the problem is that we experience 150 percent of what "normal" people do and we are frustrated that we have not yet learned how to handle it. But that does not mean that gaining control is impossible.

With incredibly hard work and the help of our entire team of supporters, we can learn to get more and more of our powers under control and actually begin to see them as unique gifts to cherish. If we assemble a team and a solid plan that takes a slow and progressive approach, we can see modest results in a short time, and accomplishments that are truly miraculous within a few years.

As we begin to learn, we gain the ability to handle more of the power available to us. Our doctors and therapists will recognize our ability to better manage our condition and can lower our medication so that it does not hold us back as much. Very slowly, and with close supervision, we can adjust our medication to the minimum needed to keep us in control. As we develop insight and make a stronger effort, our range expands and we start to experience the highs of mania and the depths of depression without losing control.

As our range expands, we are faced with new challenges that sometimes we are unable to handle. However, with proper supervision, we become much better at recognizing the edges of our abilities. Thus, we can fine tune both our medications and our efforts to help us function in a better range.

The shocking discovery came when I started learning how to see the benefits in depression. As I learned to better understand what was going on, I learned that I could function very well in a depressed state and it afforded me insights that I never dreamed were possible. The best changes we ever make in our lives are often the result of insights gained in depression. We might accomplish many things when manic, but the desires to reevaluate our lives and to make changes are not among them.

This exploration is exhilarating, but should only be explored with the help of a professional team. It will take tremendous effort and tenacity; there will be many times when it seems hopeless, as if you are making no progress or are even sliding backward. If you look back far enough, though, you can always see progress which, if kept up, will inevitably lead to success.

Along the way you will discover "super powers" you never knew you had. Best of all, you will discover yourself and realize that those powers were given to you to help you along the way. Stan Lee has often said: "With great power comes great responsibility." It is our greatest responsibility to keep our powers under control while learning to harness them for good.

Acknowledgments

Writing a book about depression is substantially harder than sitting down while manic and letting it flow. This book was one of the hardest projects I have ever taken on. I set out to write the book while in a state of depression, but writing is not one of depression's strengths. Instead of cranking out a book in a week, this one took the better part of a year to write the first draft.

Without my wife Ellen, this book would never have been finished. She encouraged me when I was ready to give up, and helped me to sort out my feelings and ideas. When it seemed impossible to even start the chapters about the saints, Ellen helped me write these chapters and made them even better than I was aiming for.

The writing in this book is much better than *The Bipolar Advantage*, yet is still far from perfect. It makes a big difference to take time and review my writing instead of aiming for speed, but the biggest change was hiring George Goddard as my editor. George pointed out so many changes that I had to learn to write better. Nick Stone then polished the final text to maximize clarity and tie up the loose ends.

When the book was in its final stages, my daughter Kate and I read the book out loud together. With this method, we were able to catch the minor errors in the book that the other editors had not seen. This process helped make the book clearer, but more importantly created an even deeper connection between us.

I got so many compliments about the cover of *The Bipolar Advantage,* that I had to talk to Don Farnsworth about the cover for this book. I had no idea what to even ask him for, but a couple of hours later, I was blown away once again by his artwork. With all of his other projects, I am so lucky that he so readily makes time to help me out. Visit www.magnoliaeditions.com to see a range of Don's projects: from giant inkjet prints combining ultrarealistic insects with chapters of Darwin's Origin of Species, to state-of-the-art Jacquard tapestries, as well as collaborative projects with blue-chip artists like Chuck Close and Bruce Conner.

Don's talented daughter, Marisha Farnsworth, brought my concepts to life by creating the three dimensional illustrations in the *Redefining Our Scale* chapter, the back cover, and the animations I use in my presentations.

My good friend Brahmachari Lee has always accepted me just the way I am. But if asked for advice, he always expects me to act like a saint. He was instrumental in the most important change in the book - the change in my own behavior. We all need friends that see the best in us. They help us to be greater than we would be if left to our own excuses.

Lee also played a central role in helping me through my own "Dark Night of the Soul." By accepting where I was and not challenging my arguments, he showed that the strength of conviction is not dependent on forcing agreement with his point of view. He knew that I had to work it out in my own time.

There are so many others who have shared their insights with me. They came to take a workshop or hear me talk, hoping to add to their own insight, but in sharing their own experiences and perceptions, they have enriched my life. I am so lucky to be able to assemble groups of people to create a positive view of the future together. If we can help each other to change ourselves, we can change the world.

Printed in the United States
92447LV00001B/154-252/A

9 780977 442324